Busy Ant Maths

Progress Guide 6

Series Editor: Peter Clarke

Authors: Linda Glithro, Elizabeth Jurgensen, Jeanette Mumford, Sandra Roberts

William Collins' dream of knowledge for all began with the publication of his first book in 1819. A self-educated mill worker, he not only enriched millions of lives, but also founded a flourishing publishing house. Today, staying true to this spirit, Collins books are packed with inspiration, innovation and practical expertise. They place you at the centre of a world of possibility and give you exactly what you need to explore it.

Collins. Freedom to teach.

Published by Collins
An imprint of HarperCollins*Publishers*
77–85 Fulham Palace Road
Hammersmith
London
W6 8JB

| Browse the complete Collins catalogue at |
| **www.collins.co.uk** |

© HarperCollins*Publishers* Limited 2014

10 9 8 7 6 5 4 3 2 1

ISBN 978-0-00-756839-0

British Library Cataloguing in Publication Data
A Catalogue record for this publication is available from the British Library

Publishing Manager: Fiona McGlade
Managing Editor: Sarah Thomas
Project editor: Mariateresa Bortoluzzi
Production: Rachel Weaver
Editors: Catherine Dakin and Cassandra Fox
Cover design and artwork: Amparo Barrera
Internal design concept: Amparo Barrera
Designed: Amanda Newman and Emma DeBanks
Illustrations: Louise Forshaw and Eva Sassin
Printed and bound by Martins the Printers Ltd, Berwick-upon-Tweed

Contents

Unit 3

Week 1: **Number – Addition and subtraction**
    Lesson 1, Support: 5-digit addition
    Lesson 2, Extension: Hit the target
    Lesson 2, Extension: Hit the target 2
    Lesson 4, Support: Book sale

Week 2: **Number – Number – Decimals**
    Lesson 1, Extension: 3000-in-a-row
    Lesson 2, Support: Move the digits
    Lesson 3, Extension: What other calculations?
    Lesson 4, Support: Rounding up or down?

Week 3: **Measurement (length)**
    Lesson 1, Support: See-saw lengths
    Lesson 2, Extension: Gerry's jumping bean
    Lesson 4, Support: Motor boat hires
    Lesson 4, Extension: Distances by air

Unit 4

Week 1: **Number – Multiplication and division**
    Lesson 1, Support: Multiples and factors
    Lesson 1, Extension: Multiples and factors
    Lesson 3, Support: Dividing ThHTO by 11 and 12 using the formal written method of short division
    Lesson 3, Extension: Dividing ThHTO by 11 and 12 using the formal written method of short division

Week 2: **Number – Fractions, incl. Decimals and percentages**
    Lesson 1, Extension: Fraction and decimal triangles
    Lesson 2, Support: One divided
    Lesson 3, Extension: 3–in-a-row
    Lesson 4, Support: Theatre percentages

Week 3: **Measurement (time)**
    Lesson 1, Support: Time dominoes
    Lesson 1, Extension: Domino times
    Lesson 2, Support: Secondary school visit
    Lesson 4, Extension: Applying units of speed

Unit 5

Week 1: **Number – Addition, subtraction, multiplication and division, incl. Number and place value**
Lesson 1, Support: Negative tug of war
Lesson 2, Extension: 4-in-a-row
Lesson 3, Support: Brackets first!
Lesson 4, Extension: Roll the dice

Week 2: **Number – Algebra**
Lesson 1, Support: Simplifying and using formulae games
Lesson 2, Extension: Investigating triangular numbers
Lesson 3, Support: Lucky numbers
Lesson 4, Extension: Designing a patio

Week 3: **Geometry – Properties of shape**
Lesson 1, Extension: 5-piece puzzle
Lesson 2, Extension: Angles in regular polygons
Lesson 2, Support: Shapes on a pinboard
Lesson 4, Support: 3-angle puzzle

Unit 6

Week 1: **Number – Multiplication and division**
Lesson 1, Support: Multiplication HTO x TO using partitioning
Lesson 3, Support: Multiplication HTO x TO using the expanded written method
Lesson 3, Extension: Multiplication HTO x TO using the expanded written method
Lesson 4, Extension: Multiplication HTO x TO using the formal written method

Week 2: **Number – Multiplication and division, incl. Decimals**
Lesson 1, Support: Multiplying decimal using mental methods
Lesson 1, Extension: Multiplying decimal using mental methods
Lesson 3, Support: Multiplying decimal by a 1-digit number
Lesson 4, Extension: Multiplying decimal by a 1-digit number using the formal written method

Week 3: **Measurement (mass)**
Lesson 1, Support: Domino grams and kilograms
Lesson 2, Support: Mass of parcels
Lesson 3, Extension: Fish figures
Lesson 4, Extension: Delivery rounds

Unit 7

Week 1: **Number – Fractions**
Lesson 1, Extension: What's the question?
Lesson 2, Support: Dividing pizzas
Lesson 3, Extension: Multiplying fraction rhyme
Lesson 4, Support: Eating pizzas

Week 2: **Ratio and proportion**
Lesson 1, Support: Flowerbeds
Lesson 2, Support: Stripy scarves
Lesson 3, Extension: Music shop ratios
Lesson 4, Extension: Best value breakfast

Week 3: **Statistics**
Lesson 1, Support: Data in pie charts
Lesson 1, Extension: Driving lessons pie chart
Lesson 4, Support: Find the mean scores
Lesson 4, Extension: 2-digit mean scores

Unit 8

Week 1: **Number – Multiplication and division**
Lesson 1, Support: Division HTO ÷ TO using the expanded written method
Lesson 2, Support: Division ThHTO ÷ TO using the expanded written method
Lesson 2, Extension: Division ThHTO ÷ TO using the expanded written method
Lesson 4, Extension: Number pathways

Week 2: **Number – Multiplication and division, incl. Decimals**
Lesson 1, Support: Dividing decimals using mental methods
Lesson 2, Support: Dividing decimals using the expanded written method of
long division
Lesson 2, Extension: Candle problems
Lesson 4, Extension: Car troubles

Week 3: **Measurement (perimeter and area)**
Lesson 1, Support: Same perimeter
Lesson 2, Extension: Investigating the area of squares
Lesson 3, Support: Dot grid area
Lesson 3, Extension: Puzzling pieces

Unit 9

Week 1: **Number - Addition and subtraction**
- Lesson 1, Support: Race to 500 000
- Lesson 2, Extension: Shape values
- Lesson 3, Support: BODAMAS rules!
- Lesson 4, Extension: Franco's chairs

Week 2: **Algebra**
- Lesson 1, Support: Collecting terms and using brackets
- Lesson 1, Extension: Serpent algebra
- Lesson 3, Support: Algebra puzzle squares
- Lesson 3, Extension: Gradients

Week 3: **Geometry – Properties of shape**
- Lesson 2, Support: Hexagon patterns
- Lesson 2, Extension: Circle designs
- Lesson 3, Support: Patterns in a circle
- Lesson 3, Extension: Egg tangrams

Unit 10

Week 1: **Number – Multiplication and division, incl. Decimals**
- Lesson 1, Support: Multiplying decimals by a 2-digit number using the grid method
- Lesson 2, Support: Multiplying decimals by a 2-digit number using the expanded written method
- Lesson 2, Extension: Multiplying decimals by a 2-digit number using the expanded written method
- Lesson 4, Extension: Solving word problems

Week 2: **Number – Fractions**
- Lesson 1, Support: Equal fractions
- Lesson 2, Extension: Charity spending
- Lesson 3, Extension: Fraction and decimal multiplication grid
- Lesson 4, Support: Share it out

Week 3: **Measurement (volume and capacity)**
- Lesson 1, Support: Decision tree litres
- Lesson 2, Extension: Water-flow rates
- Lesson 3, Support: Volume of cuboids
- Lesson 3, Extension: Investigating painted cubes

Unit 11

Week 1: **Number – Addition, subtraction, multiplication and division**
Lesson 1, Extension: BODMAS challenge
Lesson 2, Support: Make it to twenty
Lesson 3, Extension: Make the puzzle
Lesson 4, Support: Another curious question

Week 2: **Ratio and proportion**
Lesson 2, Support: Ratio generator
Lesson 4, Support: Egg ratios and proportions
Lesson 2, Extension: Paper sizes
Lesson 3, Extension: Theme park ratios

Week 3: **Geometry – Position and direction**
Lesson 1, Extension: Locate the shapes
Lesson 2, Support: Points on the run
Lesson 4, Support: On reflection
Lesson 4, Extension: 4-quadrant pattern

Unit 12

Week 1: **Number – Multiplication and division, incl. Decimals**
Lesson 1, Support: Using divisibility tests
Lesson 2, Support: Review multiplication and division of whole numbers
Lesson 2, Extension: Review multiplication and division of whole numbers
Lesson 3, Extension: Review multiplication and division involving decimal numbers

Week 2: **Number – Fractions, incl. Decimals and percentages**
Lesson 1, Support: Sale prices
Lesson 2, Extension: Slide into place
Lesson 3, Support: Point to it
Lesson 3, Extension: Cover them up

Week 3: **Statistics**
Lesson 1, Support: Premier pie charts
Lesson 4, Support: About means
Lesson 1, Extension: Pie chart survey
Lesson 4, Extension: Investigating means

Name: _____ Date: _____

-digit counting

Read and write numbers to 10 000 000 and determine the value of each digit

1 Count on or back in 100s from the numbers and write each number.

a

399 890
399 990

b

187 712

c

562 038
562 138

d

1 856 502

2 Count on or back in 1000s from the numbers and write each number.

a

736 024
737 024

b

1 827 553

c

2 575 239
2 576 239

d

3 857 320

Name: _____ Date: _____

Highest number wins

Order and compare numbers to 10 000 000
and determine the value of each digit

You will need:
• 2 x 0–9 dice

Play this game with a partner.

- Each player rolls a dice.

- Decide in which place value you are going to write the number rolled, then write it in one of the boxes.

- You can either write the number rolled in your set of boxes or in your partner's.

- Once you have written the number, it cannot be changed.

- The aim is to make a higher number than your partner's.

- Play eight rounds. The winner is the player who wins more rounds.

Player 1 _____

Player 2 _____

Name: _____ Date: _____

Round me

Round any whole number to the required degree of accuracy

Reading the number out loud to myself helps me to work out which multiples it is between.

Round these numbers to the nearest multiples of 10 and 100.

Hint

this digit tells you which multiple of 100 to round to

this digit tells you which multiple of 10 to round to

67 841

Example

tens
30 730

30 726

hundreds
30 700

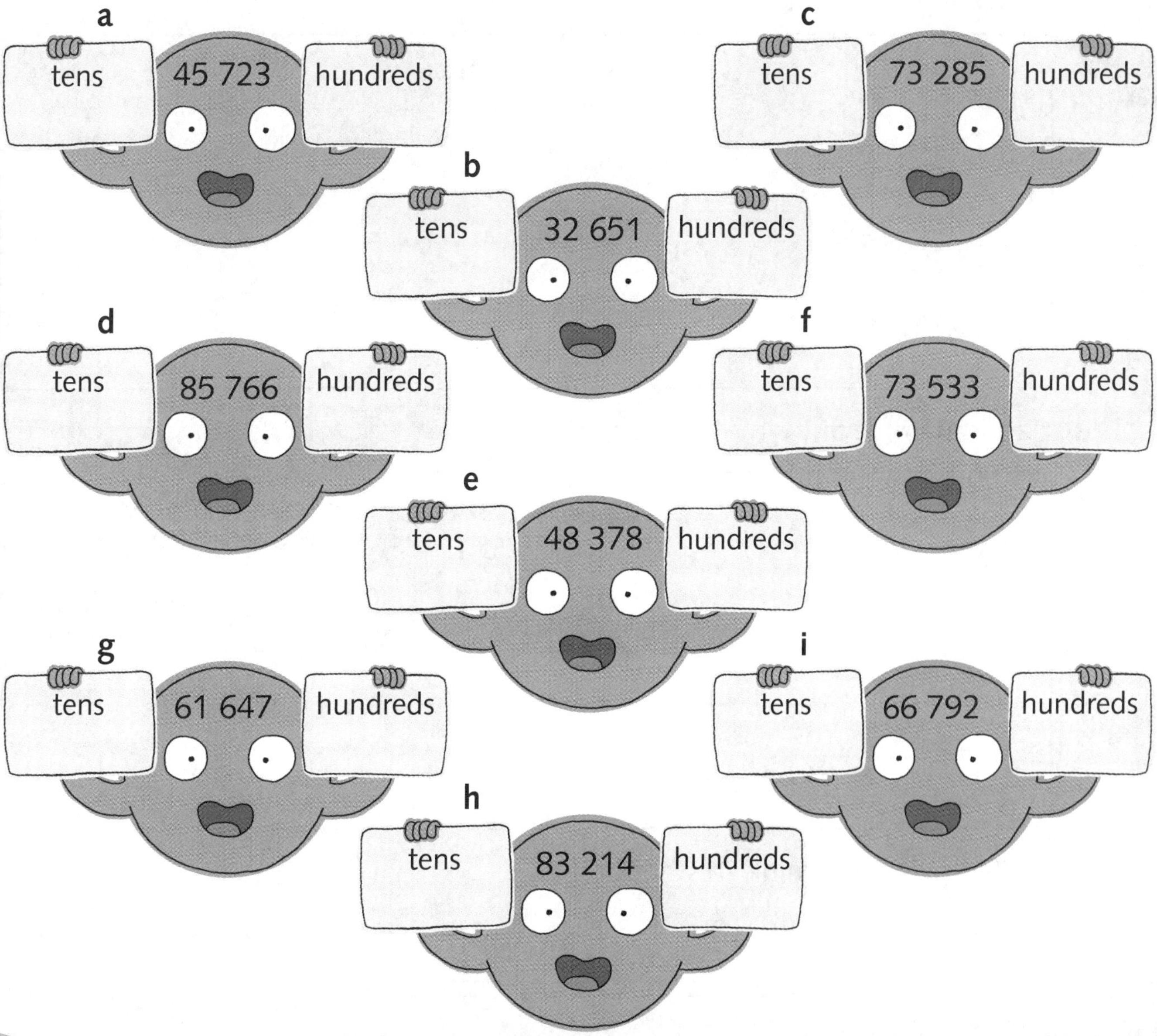

a

tens

45 723

hundreds

c

tens

73 285

hundreds

b

tens

32 651

hundreds

d

tens

85 766

hundreds

f

tens

73 533

hundreds

e

tens

48 378

hundreds

g

tens

61 647

hundreds

i

tens

66 792

hundreds

h

tens

83 214

hundreds

Name: _____ Date: _____

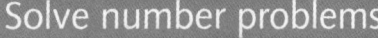

Why 11?

Solve number problems

This number is standing
at the bus stop:

If digit 6 goes to the back of the
queue, the new number will be:

1 Add the two numbers above together. Is the answer a multiple of 11?

_____

2 Try adding two different 6-digit numbers. Check the answer is also a
multiple of 11.

Working out

3 Can you work out why this happens?

Working out

Hint

5000 is not divisible by 11.
5005 is divisible by 11.

200 000 is not divisible by 11.
200 002 is divisible by 11.

4 Explain why you think this happens.

_____

_____

Name: _____ Date: _____

Number chain

Add mentally, including with large numbers

Write the missing numbers to complete the number chain.

Start

1 276 309 + [ ] = 1 476 309 + [ ]

1 481 309 + [ ] = 1 505 309 + [ ]

2 105 309 + [ ] = 2 105 959 + [ ]

2 148 959 + [ ] = 3 048 959 + [ ]

3 056 959 + [ ] = 3 058 059 + [ ]

3 060 559 + [ ] = 3 065 059 + [ ]

Finish

Subtraction number lines

Subtract mentally, including large numbers

Use the number lines to work out these calculations. The digits you need to focus on are in bold.

Example   268 400 – 4300

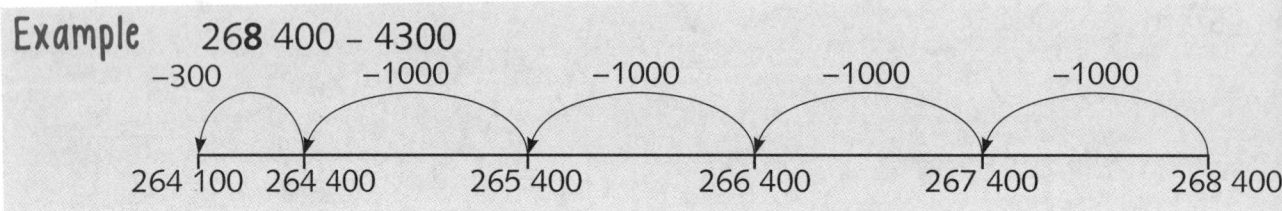

-300 -1000 -1000 -1000 -1000

264 100   264 400   265 400   266 400   267 400   268 400

a 4**72** 648 – 8600

b **382** 204 – 6500

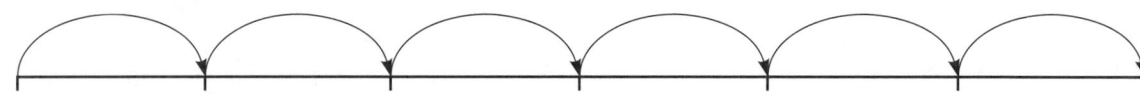

c **581** 729 – 4700

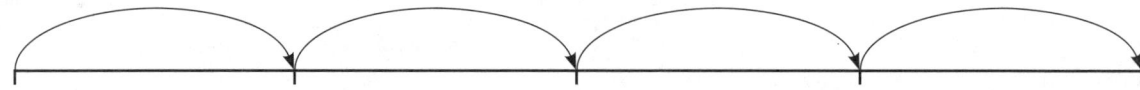

d 241 **633** – 510

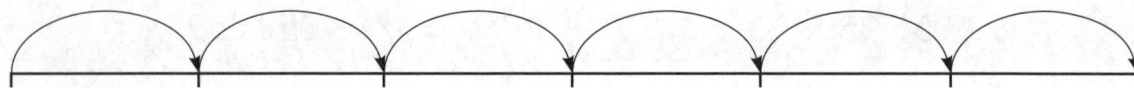

e 673 104 – 42 000

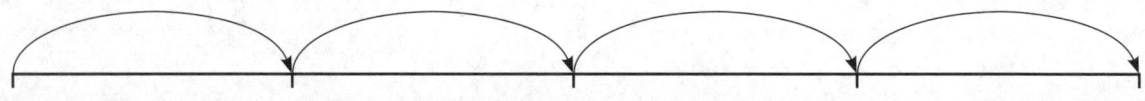

Name: _____ Date: _____

Decimal puzzles

Add and subtract decimals mentally

The decimal numbers on each side of the square total the number in the circle.

- Choose a number to go in the centre circle.

- Fill in the boxes around the circle with decimals with 1 and 2 places so that the three boxes on each side of the diamond add up to your middle number.

- Copy out your puzzles with some of the numbers missing.

- Give them to your partner to complete.

Your complete puzzles

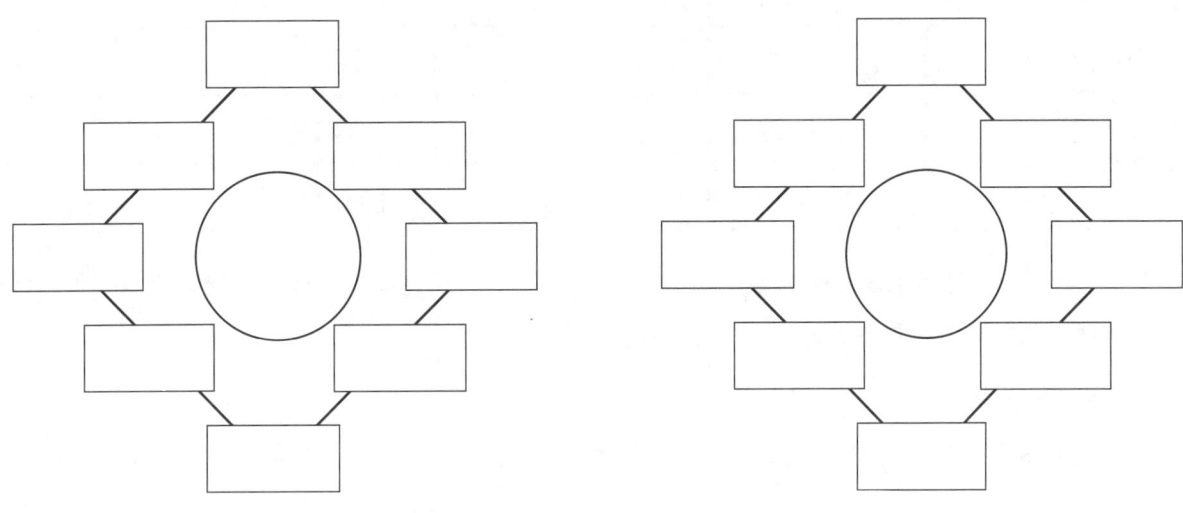

- ✂

Puzzles for your partner

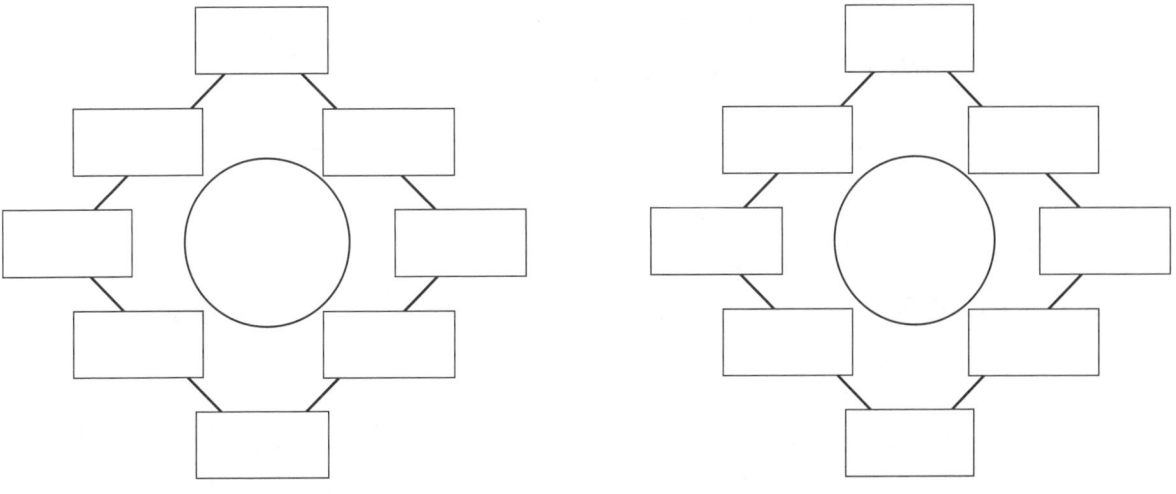

Name: _____ Date: _____

Museum figures

- Solve multi-step problems in contexts, deciding which operations and methods to use and why
- Use estimation to check accuracy of answers

Type of museum	Half-yearly visitor numbers	Numbers rounded to the nearest 1000	Next year's targets	Increase
Science	469 720		495 000	
Natural History	725 104		825 000	
Maritime	231 539		240 000	
Local History	82 935		90 000	
Transport	108 322		128 000	
Childhood	133 800		150 000	
Farm	53 067		70 000	
War	104 493		114 000	

1 Round all the half-yearly visitor numbers to the nearest 1000 and write them in the third column.

2 What is the increase between the rounded figures and next year's targets? Write the numbers in the Increase column of the table below.

3 Which type of museum has the largest target increase?

4 Use the rounded sales numbers to work out the total number of visitors to the War and Farm museums.

5 Use the rounded sales numbers to estimate the difference between the most and least popular museums.

6 The Maritime Museum gave out 15 000 free tickets over the year. How many visitors had to pay to enter?

7 On the back of this sheet, make up two questions of your own about the museums.

Name: _____ Date: _____

dentifying nets

Identify different nets for an open cube

You will need:
• scissors

1 Carefully cut out the shapes along the dashed lines (------).
   Fold up each shape along the dotted lines (.....) to find which nets are for
   open cubes. The black square is the base of the shape.

2 Complete the table. Enter ✓ if the shape is a net of an open cube and
   ✗ if it is not.

Shape	A	B	C	D	E	F
Net of an open cube						

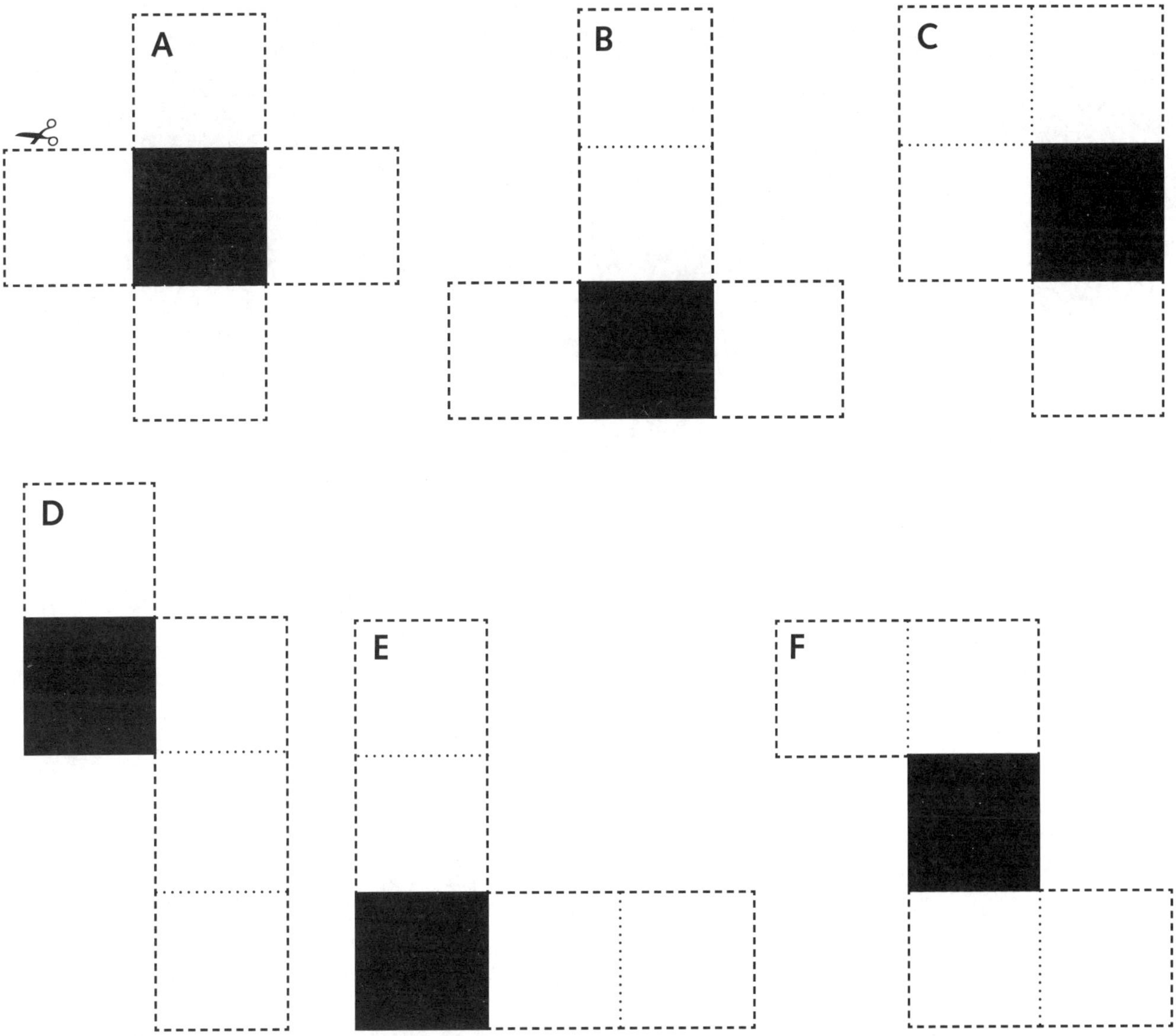

A

B

C

D

E

F

Name: _____ Date: _____

2-piece puzzle

Construct nets for a cube

You will need:
- ruler
- scissors
- glue

Work with a partner to each make a 3-D shape from the net.

- Cut out the net.
  Score along the dotted lines before folding.
  Fold up the net to visualise the 3-D shape.
  Stick the tabs, in turn, beginning with tab 1.

- Join the two shapes you have both
  made to make a cube.

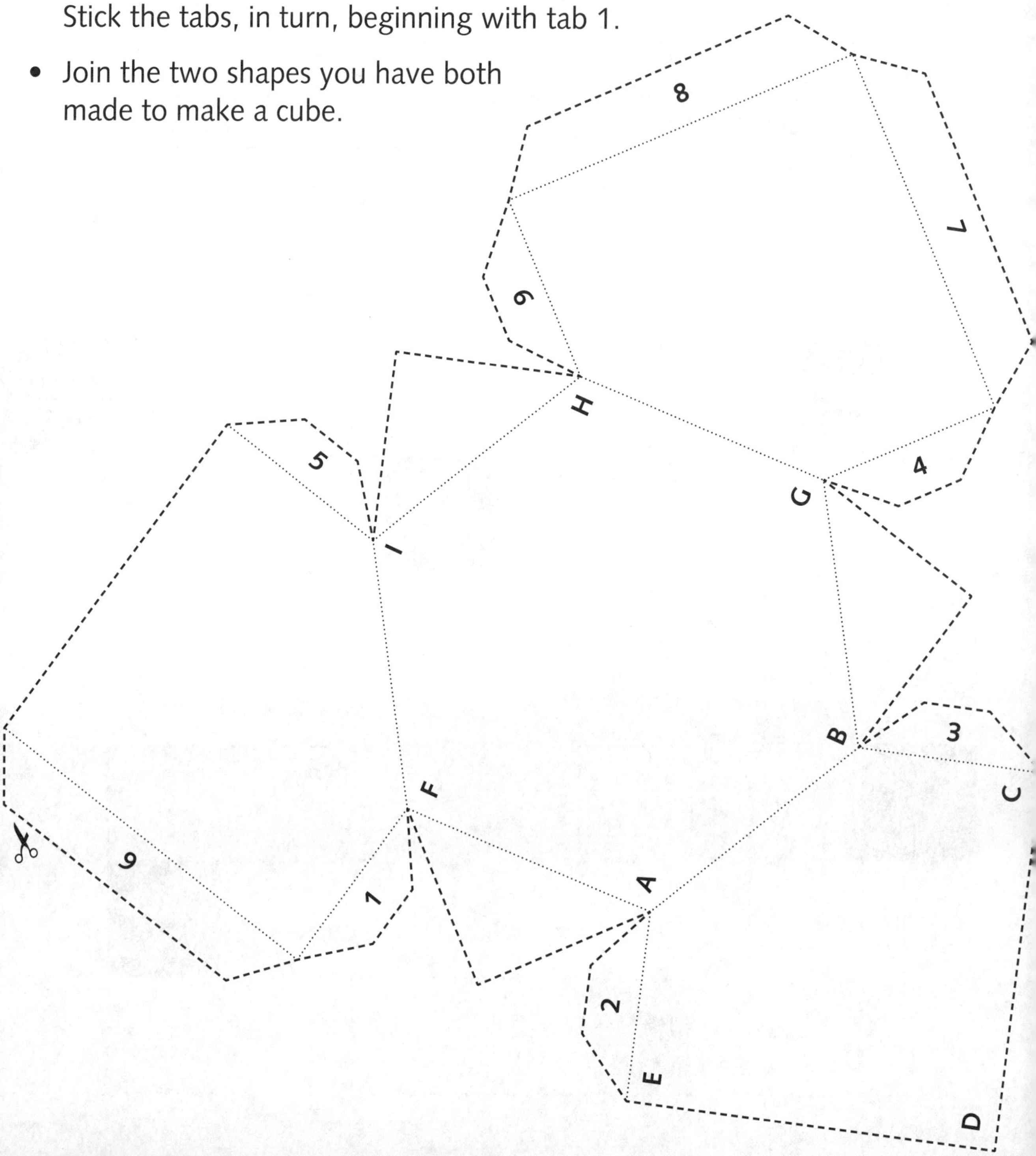

Name: _____ Date: _____

Net of a triangular prism

Draw nets for shapes with one or more triangular faces

You will need:
- two triangular and three rectangular interlocking tiles
- scissors
- ruler
- glue

- Use your interlocking tiles to build a triangular prism.

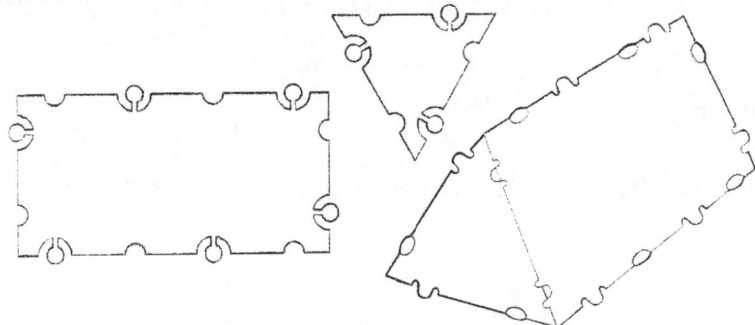

- Use your triangular prism to help you complete the net of the triangular prism below.

- Draw the tabs on your second triangle, then cut out the net and glue the shape together.

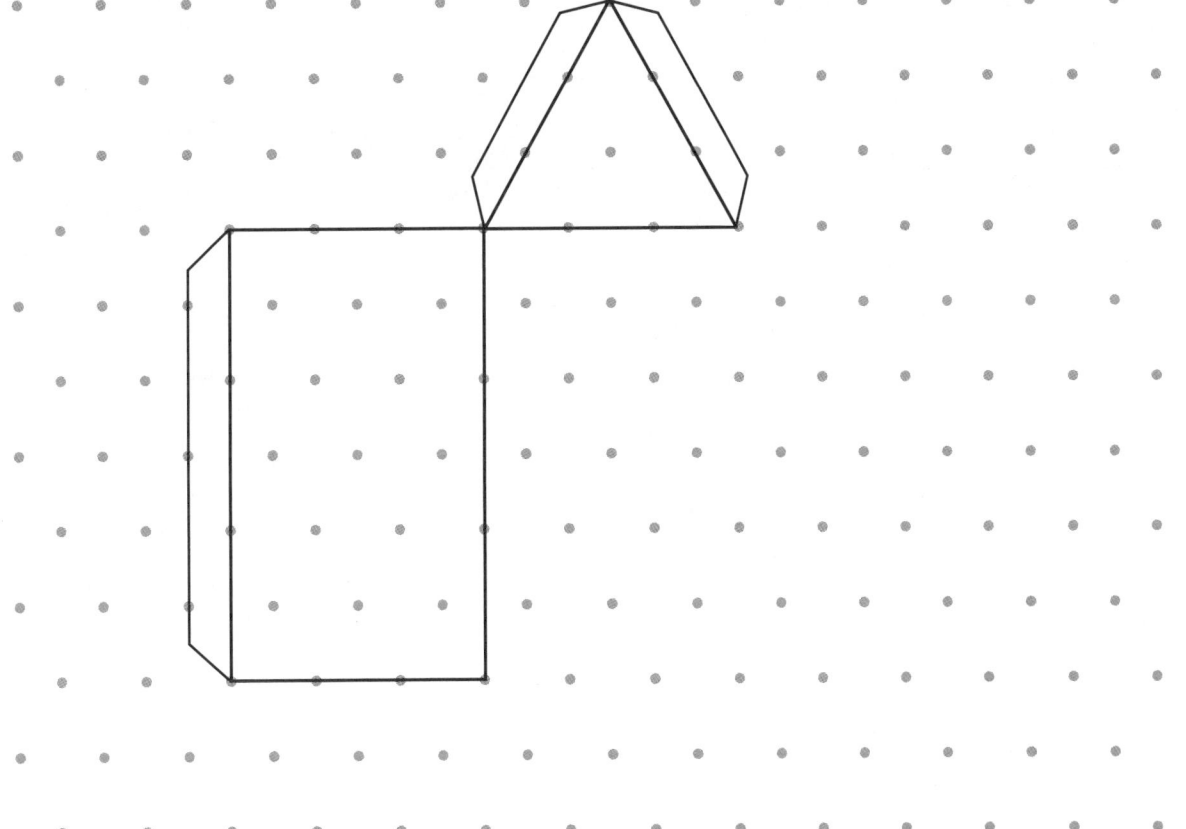

Name: _____ Date: _____

Cubes from square-based pyramids

Draw nets for shapes with one or more triangular faces

You will need:
• scissors
• ruler
• glue

Work with a partner.

- Each person cuts out and assembles the three nets of a square-based pyramid.

- Using all six square-based pyramids, find a way to put them together to form a cube.

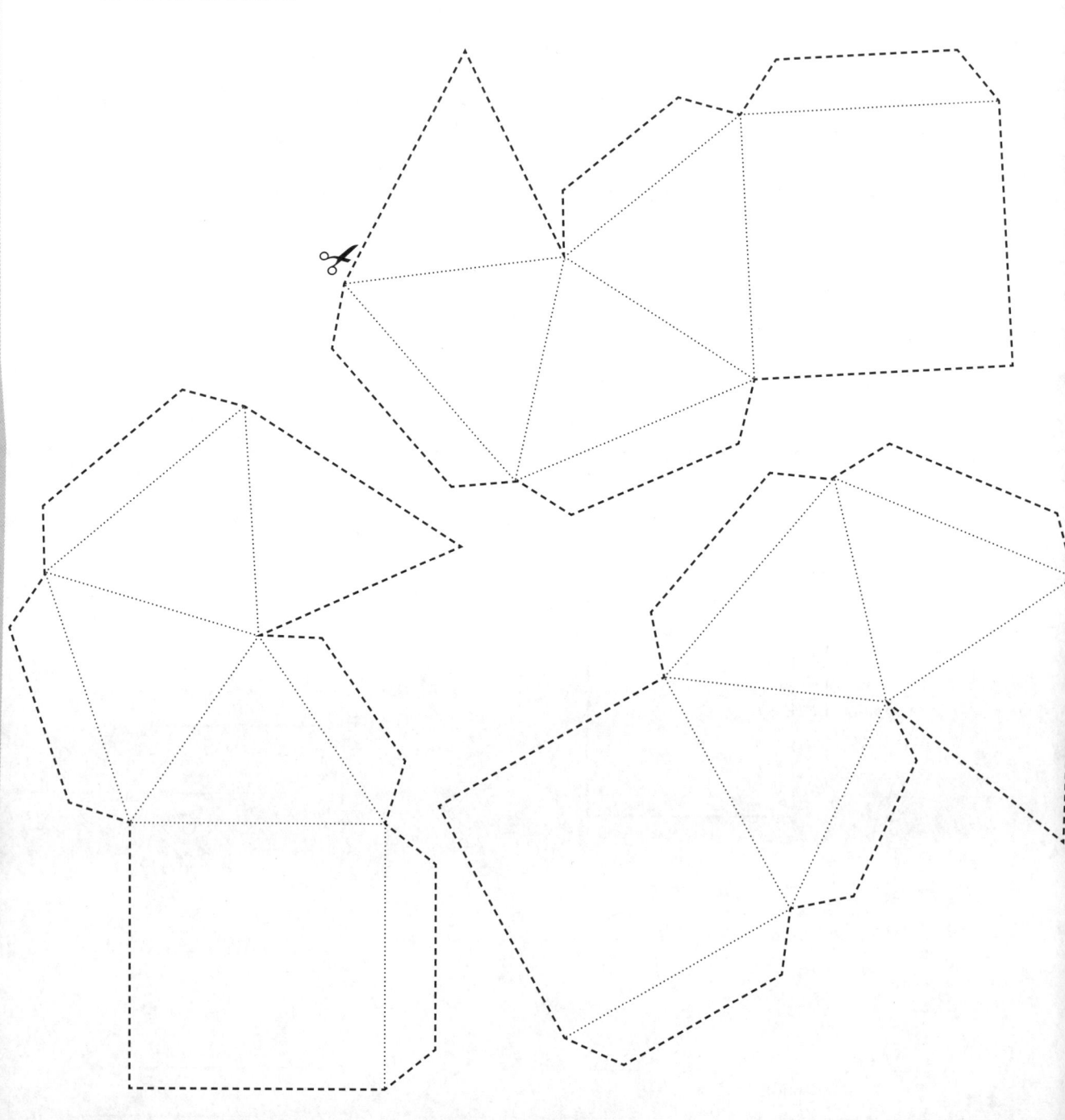

Name: _____ Date: _____

Multiplying ThHTO x O

- Use the formal written method of short multiplication to calculate ThHTO × O
- Estimate and check the answer to a calculation

1 Find the approximate answer to each calculation.

2 Work out the answer to each calculation using the formal written method.

3 Check your answer is close to your estimated answer.

Example

$3273 \times 7 \rightarrow 3000 \times 7 = 21\,000$

TTh	Th	H	T	O
	3	2	7	3
X	1	5	2	7
2	2	9	1	1

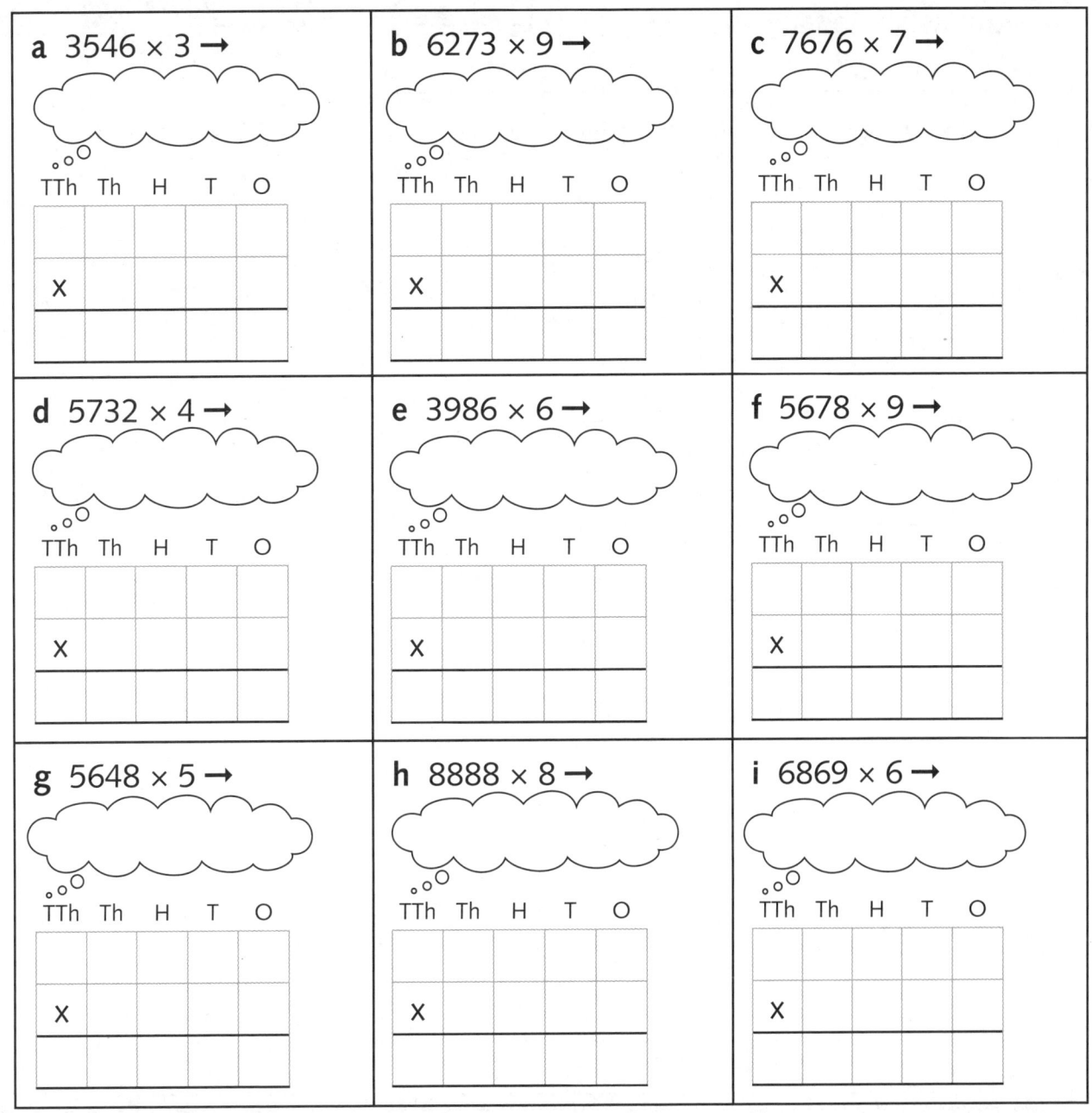

a 3546 × 3 →

TTh Th H T O

X

b 6273 × 9 →

TTh Th H T O

X

c 7676 × 7 →

TTh Th H T O

X

d 5732 × 4 →

TTh Th H T O

X

e 3986 × 6 →

TTh Th H T O

X

f 5678 × 9 →

TTh Th H T O

X

g 5648 × 5 →

TTh Th H T O

X

h 8888 × 8 →

TTh Th H T O

X

i 6869 × 6 →

TTh Th H T O

X

Name: _____ Date: _____

Multiplying TO x TO using the expanded written method

- Use the expanded written method to calculate TO × TO
- Estimate and check the answer to a calculation

1 Find the approximate answer to each calculation.

2 Work out the answer to each calculation using the expanded written method. Choose the method from the Example box that you prefer.

3 Check your answer is close to your estimated answer.

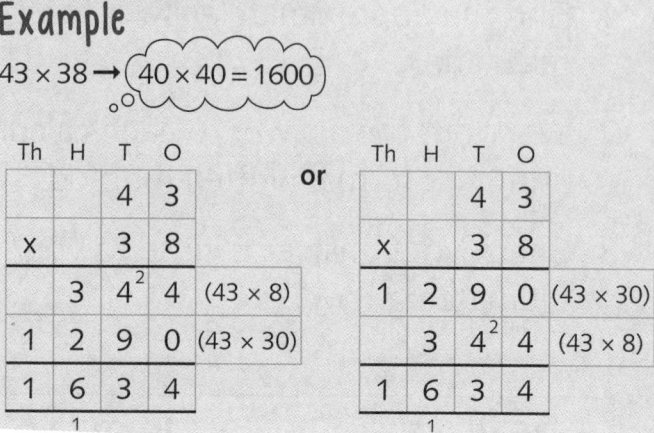

Example

$43 \times 38 \rightarrow$ $40 \times 40 = 1600$

Th	H	T	O			Th	H	T	O	
		4	3	**or**				4	3	
×		3	8			×		3	8	
	3	4²	4	(43 × 8)		1	2	9	0	(43 × 30)
1	2	9	0	(43 × 30)			3	4²	4	(43 × 8)
1	6	3	4			1	6	3	4	
		1						1		

---

a 63 × 39 →

$60 \times 40 = 2400$

Th	H	T	O	
		6	3	
×		3	9	
				(63 ×)
				(63 ×)

b 459 × 27 →

Th	H	T	O
×			

c 54 × 24 →

Th	H	T	O
×			

d 73 × 36 →

Th	H	T	O
×			

e 86 × 45 →

Th	H	T	O
×			

f 65 × 58 →

Th	H	T	O
×			

Name: _____ Date: _____

ultiplying TO x TO using the formal written method

Use the formal written method of long multiplication to calculate TO × TO

- For each pyramid, multiply the numbers next to each other on the bottom row to make the numbers on the next row.
- Repeat for each row until you reach the total at the top, using mental or the formal written methods to find each answer. Use the back of this sheet for your working.

Example

		4	6
x		3	8
	3	6⁴	8
1	3¹	8	0
1	7	4	8
	1		

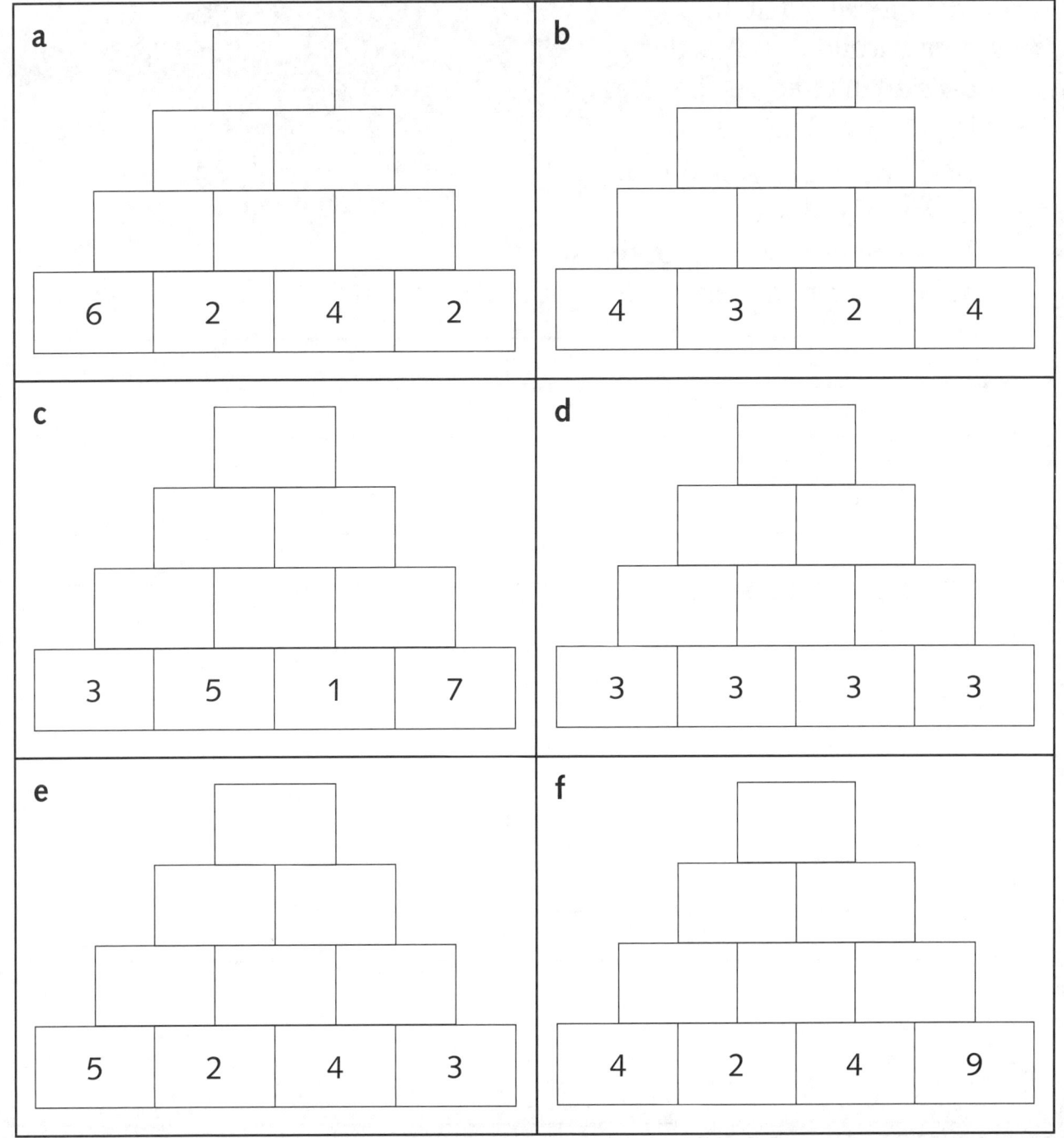

a

| 6 | 2 | 4 | 2 |

b

| 4 | 3 | 2 | 4 |

c

| 3 | 5 | 1 | 7 |

d

| 3 | 3 | 3 | 3 |

e

| 5 | 2 | 4 | 3 |

f

| 4 | 2 | 4 | 9 |

Name: _____ Date: _____

Solving word problems

Solve problems involving addition, subtraction, multiplication and division

1 The Williams family are going on holiday. Use the picture on the right to help you write your own word problems below about what they spend at the airport. Try to include calculations that involve addition, multiplication, subtraction, division or even percentages in your word problems.

AIRPORT TERMINAL

Duty free shop

£56

£48

32 kg

£14

£76

£26

2 Give your word problems to a partner to solve.
They can use the back of this sheet to write their answers. Then check their answers.

Name: _____ Date: _____

ive simplifications challenge

Use common factors to simplify fractions

1 Find a fraction that can be simplified using five simplifications.

Example

$\frac{42}{60} \rightarrow$ dividing the numerator and denominator by 2, it gives $\frac{21}{30}$

$\frac{21}{30} \rightarrow$ dividing the numerator and denominator by 3, it gives $\frac{7}{10}$

Hint

Divide the numerator and denominator by the lowest common factor each time.

I thought $\frac{42}{60}$ would need more than two simplifications.

$\dfrac{}{} = \dfrac{}{} = \dfrac{}{} = \dfrac{}{} = \dfrac{}{} = \dfrac{}{}$

$\dfrac{}{} = \dfrac{}{} = \dfrac{}{} = \dfrac{}{} = \dfrac{}{} = \dfrac{}{}$

$\dfrac{}{} = \dfrac{}{} = \dfrac{}{} = \dfrac{}{} = \dfrac{}{} = \dfrac{}{}$

$\dfrac{}{} = \dfrac{}{} = \dfrac{}{} = \dfrac{}{} = \dfrac{}{} = \dfrac{}{}$

2 Explain how you approached this problem.

_____

_____

_____

Name: _____ Date: _____

Common denominators

Use common multiples to express fractions in the same denominator

For each pair of fractions:

- write the multiples of each denominator until you find a common denominator
- circle the common denominator
- convert the fractions so they both have this denominator.

Example

$\frac{3}{4}$ | 4 | 8 | (12) | 16 | $\frac{3}{4} \overset{\times 3}{=} \frac{9}{12}$ $\times 3$

$\frac{2}{6}$ | 6 | (12) | 18 | 24 | $\frac{2}{6} \overset{\times 2}{=} \frac{4}{12}$ $\times 2$

a $\frac{1}{2}$ | 2 | 4 | 6 | 8 | $\frac{1}{2} = \square$

$\frac{5}{8}$ | $\square$ | $\square$ | $\square$ | $\square$ | $\frac{5}{8} = \square$

b $\frac{4}{9}$ | $\square$ | $\square$ | $\square$ | $\square$ | $\frac{4}{9} = \square$

$\frac{5}{6}$ | $\square$ | $\square$ | $\square$ | $\square$ | $\frac{5}{6} = \square$

c $\frac{5}{8}$ | $\square$ | $\square$ | $\square$ | $\square$ | $\frac{5}{8} = \square$

$\frac{3}{4}$ | $\square$ | $\square$ | $\square$ | $\square$ | $\frac{3}{4} = \square$

d $\frac{1}{3}$ | $\square$ | $\square$ | $\square$ | $\square$ | $\frac{1}{3} = \square$

$\frac{7}{12}$ | $\square$ | $\square$ | $\square$ | $\square$ | $\frac{7}{12} = \square$

e $\frac{4}{6}$ | $\square$ | $\square$ | $\square$ | $\square$ | $\frac{4}{6} = \square$

$\frac{7}{9}$ | $\square$ | $\square$ | $\square$ | $\square$ | $\frac{7}{9} = \square$

f $\frac{2}{3}$ | $\square$ | $\square$ | $\square$ | $\square$ | $\frac{2}{3} = \square$

$\frac{1}{4}$ | $\square$ | $\square$ | $\square$ | $\square$ | $\frac{1}{4} = \square$

g $\frac{3}{4}$ | $\square$ | $\square$ | $\square$ | $\square$ | $\frac{3}{4} = \square$

$\frac{2}{3}$ | $\square$ | $\square$ | $\square$ | $\square$ | $\frac{2}{3} = \square$

h $\frac{3}{8}$ | $\square$ | $\square$ | $\square$ | $\square$ | $\frac{3}{8} = \square$

$\frac{4}{12}$ | $\square$ | $\square$ | $\square$ | $\square$ | $\frac{4}{12} = \square$

i $\frac{5}{6}$ | $\square$ | $\square$ | $\square$ | $\square$ | $\frac{5}{6} = \square$

$\frac{6}{8}$ | $\square$ | $\square$ | $\square$ | $\square$ | $\frac{6}{8} = \square$

j $\frac{10}{12}$ | $\square$ | $\square$ | $\square$ | $\square$ | $\frac{10}{12} = \square$

$\frac{2}{3}$ | $\square$ | $\square$ | $\square$ | $\square$ | $\frac{2}{3} = \square$

k $\frac{5}{9}$ | $\square$ | $\square$ | $\square$ | $\square$ | $\frac{5}{9} = \square$

$\frac{2}{3}$ | $\square$ | $\square$ | $\square$ | $\square$ | $\frac{2}{3} = \square$

l $\frac{4}{6}$ | $\square$ | $\square$ | $\square$ | $\square$ | $\frac{4}{6} = \square$

$\frac{2}{3}$ | $\square$ | $\square$ | $\square$ | $\square$ | $\frac{2}{3} = \square$

Name: _____ Date: _____

raction combinations

Add fractions with different denominators, using the concept of equivalent fractions

- Use the digits below to make additions with three fractions.
- How many different answers can you make?
- Make sure you use all the digits in each calculation.

The fractions can be proper or improper.

$$\boxed{3} \quad \boxed{4} \quad \boxed{5} \quad \boxed{6} \quad \boxed{7} \quad \boxed{8}$$

$\dfrac{\square}{\square} + \dfrac{\square}{\square} + \dfrac{\square}{\square} = \boxed{}$

$\dfrac{\square}{\square} + \dfrac{\square}{\square} + \dfrac{\square}{\square} = \boxed{}$

$\dfrac{\square}{\square} + \dfrac{\square}{\square} + \dfrac{\square}{\square} = \boxed{}$

$\dfrac{\square}{\square} + \dfrac{\square}{\square} + \dfrac{\square}{\square} = \boxed{}$

$\dfrac{\square}{\square} + \dfrac{\square}{\square} + \dfrac{\square}{\square} = \boxed{}$

$\dfrac{\square}{\square} + \dfrac{\square}{\square} + \dfrac{\square}{\square} = \boxed{}$

$\dfrac{\square}{\square} + \dfrac{\square}{\square} + \dfrac{\square}{\square} = \boxed{}$

$\dfrac{\square}{\square} + \dfrac{\square}{\square} + \dfrac{\square}{\square} = \boxed{}$

$\dfrac{\square}{\square} + \dfrac{\square}{\square} + \dfrac{\square}{\square} = \boxed{}$

$\dfrac{\square}{\square} + \dfrac{\square}{\square} + \dfrac{\square}{\square} = \boxed{}$

Name: _____ Date: _____

Fraction subtraction

Subtract fractions and mixed numbers

Subtract these fractions using the diagrams to help you. Reduce all fractions to their simplest form.

Example

$1\frac{3}{4} - \frac{5}{4} = \frac{1}{2}$

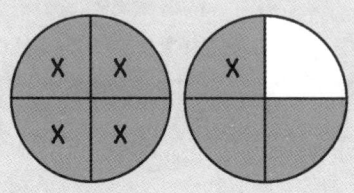

a $1\frac{2}{5} - \frac{4}{5} = \square$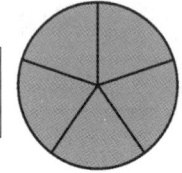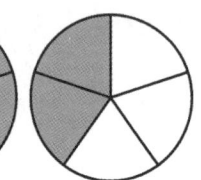

b $\frac{12}{8} - \frac{3}{4} = \square$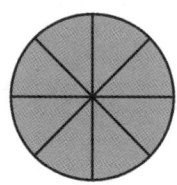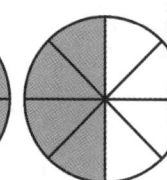

c $\frac{9}{6} - \frac{2}{3} = \square$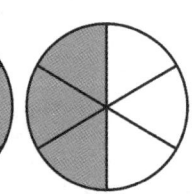

d $1\frac{4}{7} - \frac{5}{7} = \square$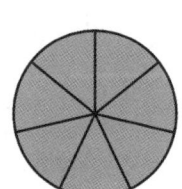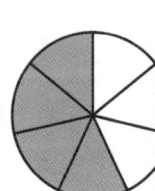

e $\frac{5}{4} - \frac{1}{2} = \square$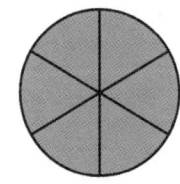

f $\frac{15}{10} - \frac{3}{5} = \square$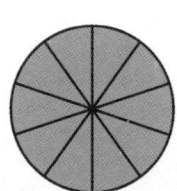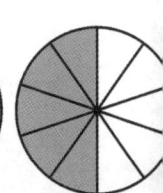

g $1\frac{1}{4} - \frac{3}{8} = \square$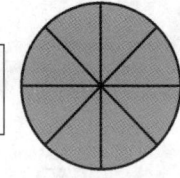

h $1\frac{6}{7} - \frac{4}{7} = \square$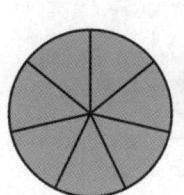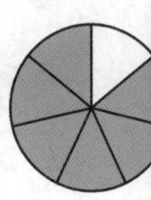

i $1\frac{2}{3} - \frac{4}{3} = \square$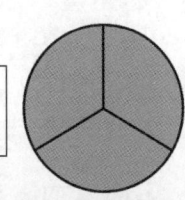

j $1\frac{3}{5} - 1\frac{1}{5} = \square$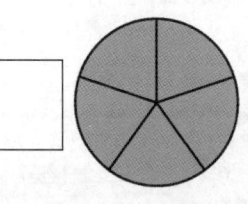

Name: _____ Date: _____

-in-a-row coordinates

Use coordinates to describe positions in two quadrants

You will need:
• counters in two colours
• two blank dice or cubes in different colours

Play this game with a partner.

- Take turns to roll both dice and put a counter on the coordinates shown by the dice.

- If the coordinates already have:
  - your partner's colour counter, you miss a turn
  - your own colour counter, roll the dice again.

- The winner is the first player to have three counters in a row, horizontally, vertically or diagonally.

Example

Number the faces of the
x-axis cube: 2, 1, 0, −1, −2, −3
y-axis cube: 0, 1, 2, 3, 4, 5.

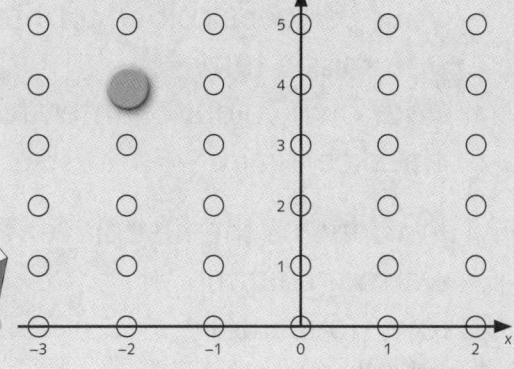

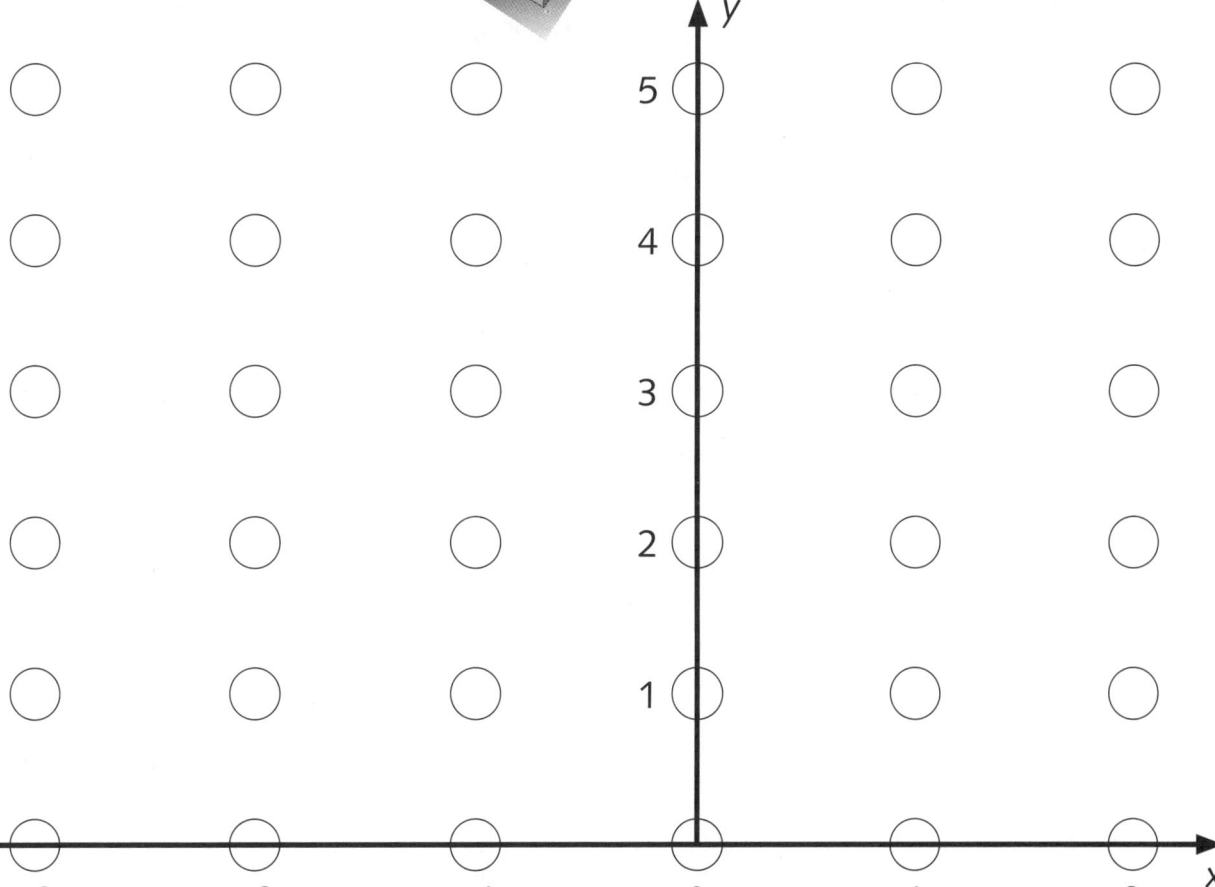

Name: _____ Date: _____

4-in-a-row coordinates

Use coordinates to describe positions in four quadrants

You will need:
- counters in two colours
- two blank dice or cubes in different colours

Play this game with a partner.

- Take turns to roll both dice and put a counter on the coordinates shown by the dice.

- If the coordinates already have:
  - your partner's colour counter, you miss a turn
  - your own colour counter, roll the dice again.

- The winner is the first player to have four counters in a row, horizontally, vertically or diagonally.

Example

Number the faces of the
x-axis cube: 2, 1, 0, −1, −2, −3
y-axis cube: 2, 1, 0, −1, −2, −3.

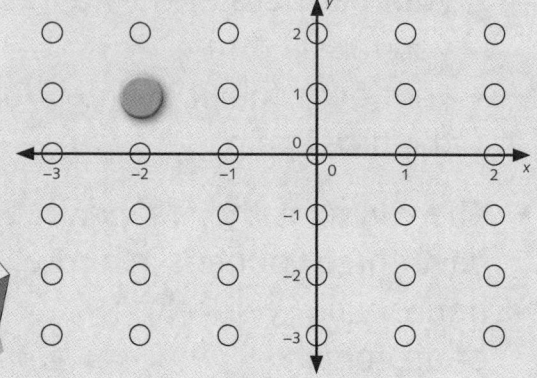

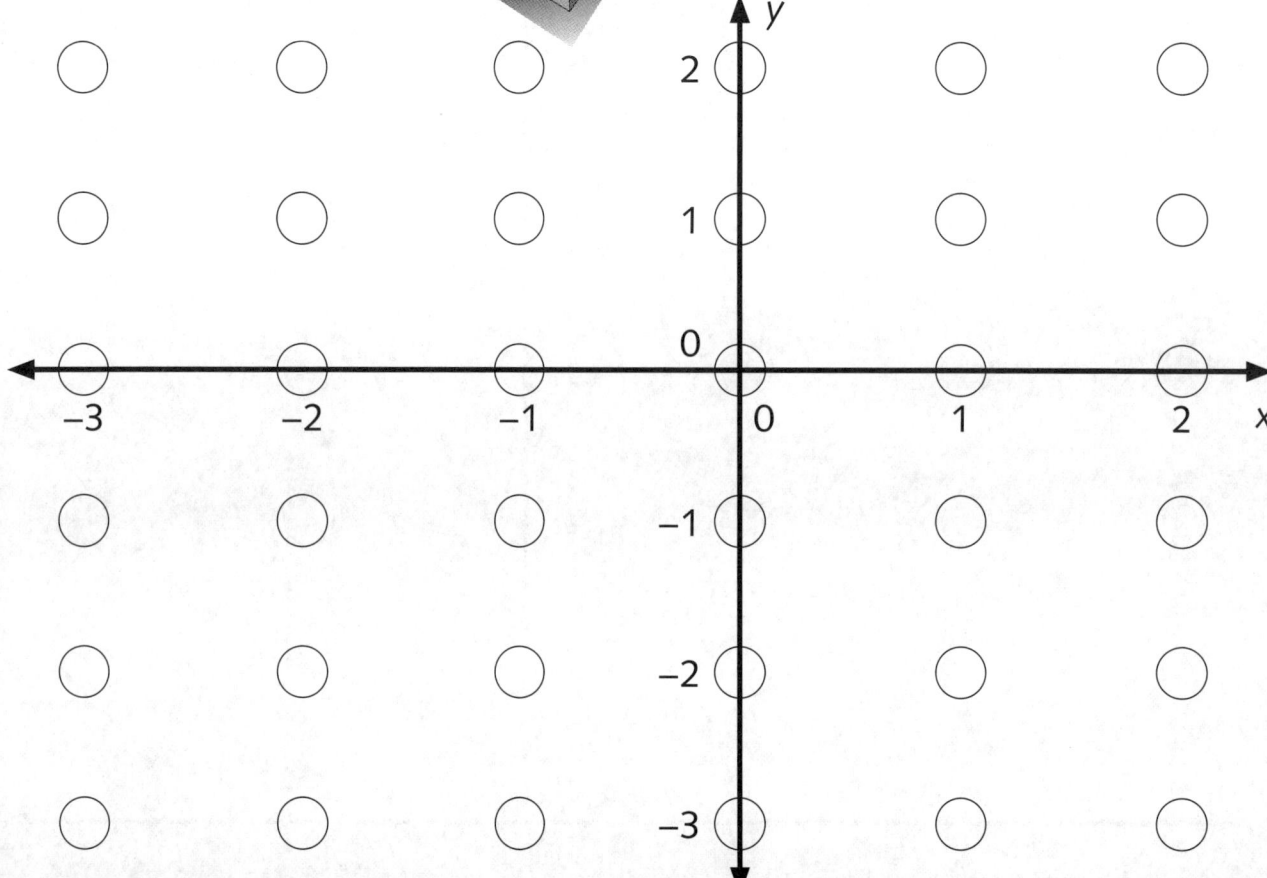

Name: _____ Date: _____

unt the square

Plot squares in the four quadrants and predict missing coordinates

Play this game with a partner.

You will need:
• ruler
• red, blue and green pencils

• Each player has a copy of this sheet. They draw a square so that it lies wholly within one of the quadrants of their grid and keep it hidden.

• Players take turns to give the coordinates of a point.

• The other player responds with one of the following:

Vertex hit	Hit	Miss
The coordinates mark a vertex of the square.	The coordinates lie on the perimeter or within the square.	The coordinates are not part of the square.

• Players mark their partner's response using a red pencil for a vertex hit, a blue pencil for a perimeter hit and a green pencil for a miss.

• Players continue, taking turns to give the coordinates to find the vertices of their partner's hidden square.

The winner is the first player to find all the vertices of their partner's square.

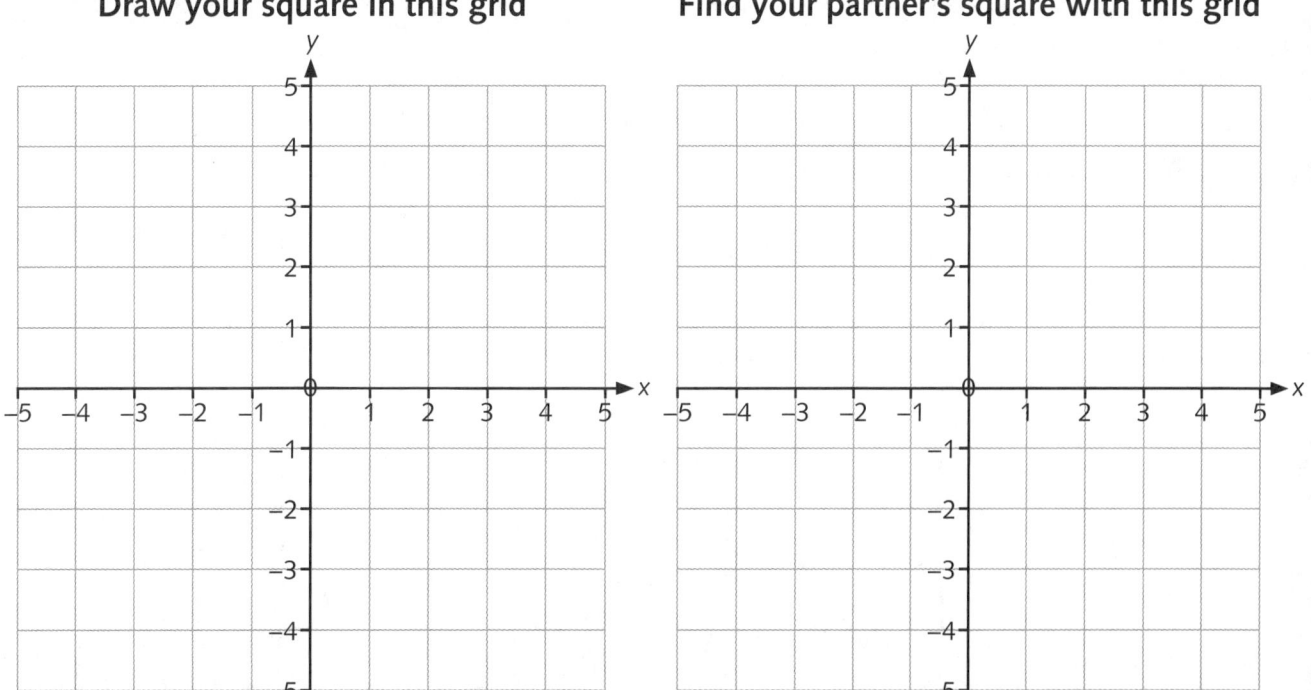

Draw your square in this grid

Find your partner's square with this grid

Name: _____ Date: _____

Hunt the rectangle

Plot rectangles in the four quadrants and predict missing coordinates

Play this game with a partner.

You will need:
- ruler
- red, blue and green pencils

- Each player draws a rectangle on their grid and keeps it hidden. A rectangle can be drawn with vertices in more than one quadrant.

- Players take turns to give the coordinates of a point.

- The other player responds with one of the following:

Vertex hit	Hit	Miss
The coordinates mark a vertex of the rectangle.	The coordinates lie on the perimeter or within the rectangle.	The coordinates are not part of the rectangle.

- Players mark their partner's response using a red pencil for a vertex hit, a blue pencil for a perimeter hit and a green pencil for a miss.

- Players continue, taking turns to give the coordinates to find the vertices of their partner's hidden rectangle.

The winner is the first player to find all the vertices of their partner's rectangle.

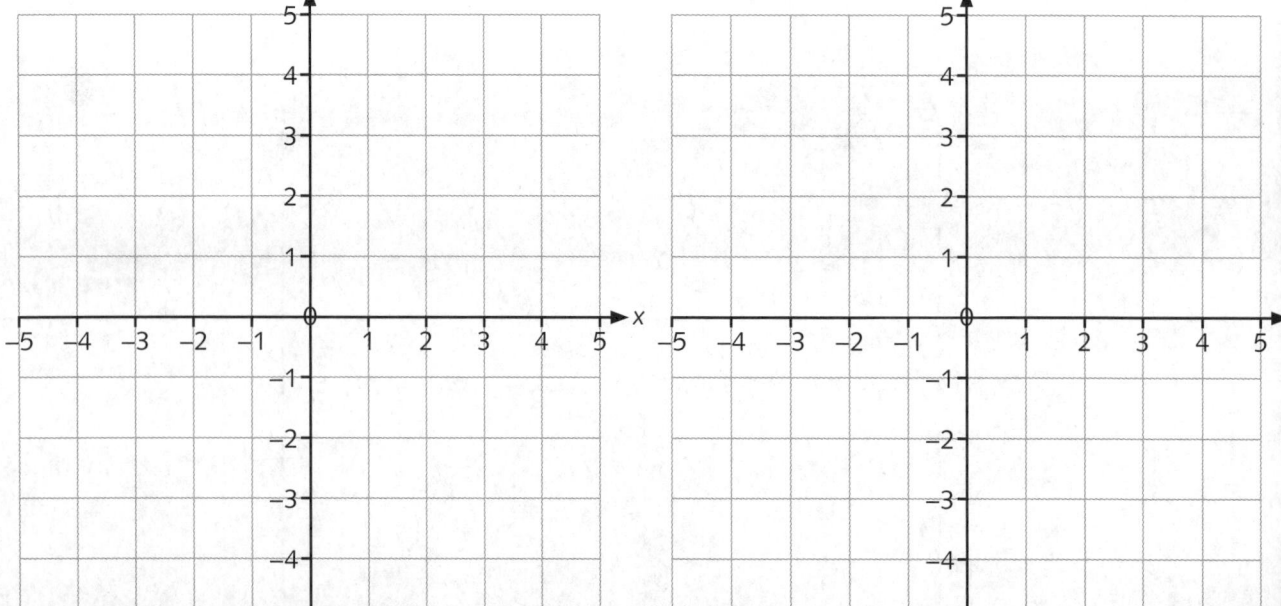

Draw your rectangle in this grid   Find your partner's rectangle with this grid

Name: _____ Date: _____

-digit addition

Add whole numbers using the formal written method
of columnar addition

Add these 5-digit numbers.

Example

```
    5  6  3  2  8
 +  2  7  1  4  3
    8  3  4  7  1
       1        1
```

a
```
   6  5  2  8  7
+  2  1  9  0  5
```

b
```
   3  3  6  3  8
+  4  8  2  4  6
```

c
```
   1  7  8  5  2
+  2  7  5  3  3
```

d
```
   4  5  2  8  6
+  2  1  8  0  8
```

e
```
   5  2  3  9  7
+  3  9  5  4  2
```

f
```
   6  3  4  9  8
+  2  5  7  2  1
```

g
```
   5  8  2  6  1
+  3  6  3  9  5
```

h
```
   4  4  8  2  5
+  5  7  0  3  7
```

i
```
   6  8  3  6  4
+  2  9  2  8  2
```

j
```
   7  3  2  9  4
+  2  2  9  0  7
```

k
```
   5  4  3  2  1
+  1  8  8  4  5
```

l
```
   8  1  3  9  5
+  1  5  2  6  7
```

Name: _____ Date: _____

Hit the target (1)

Subtract whole numbers using the formal
written method of columnar subtraction

You will need:
• 0–9 dice

- Roll the dice four times and write the digits rolled in the
  boxes below.

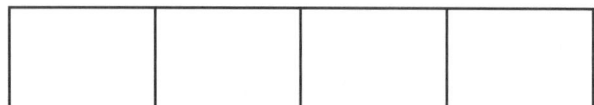

- Using only these digits (you can use each digit more
  than once), complete the subtraction calculations below.

- Your target is to have answers as close to 3 000 000
  as possible.

- After you have completed eight calculations, circle the calculation with the
  answer that is closest to 2 000 000.

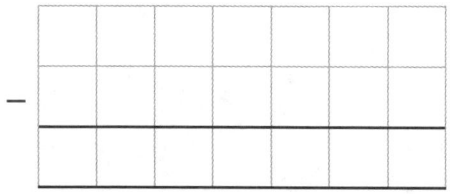
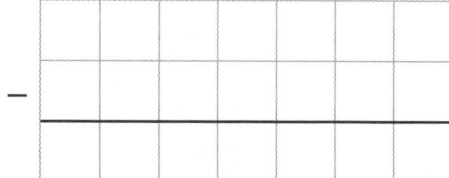

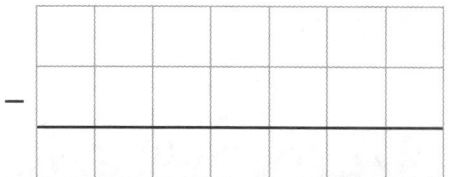
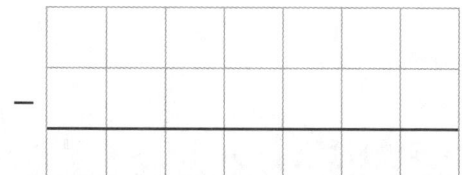

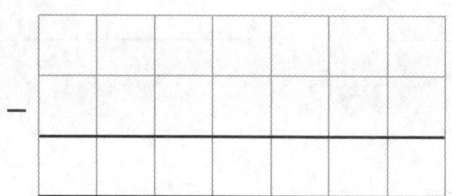
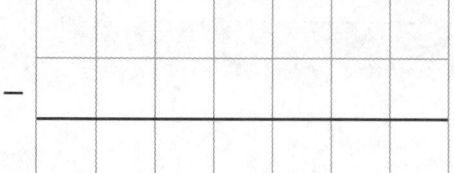

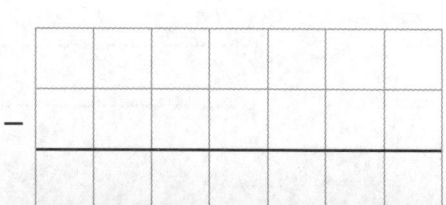

Name: _____ Date: _____

it the target (2)

Add decimals using the formal written method
of columnar addition

You will need:
• 0–9 dice

- Roll the dice six times and write the digits rolled
  in the boxes below.

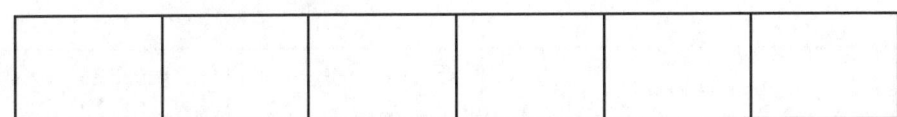

44 444·4

- Using only these digits (you can use each digit more
  than once), complete the addition calculations below.

- Your target is to have answers as close to 44 444·4
  as possible.

- After you have completed eight calculations, circle the calculation with the
  answer that is closest to 44 444.4.

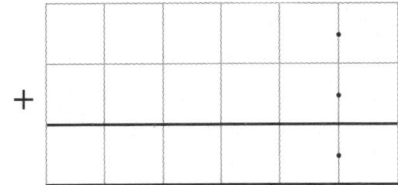

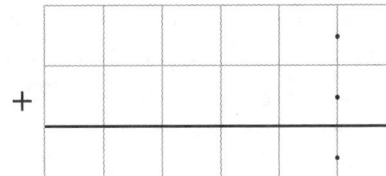

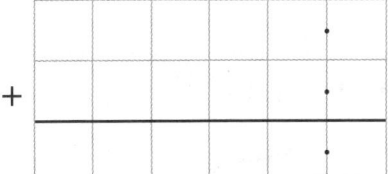

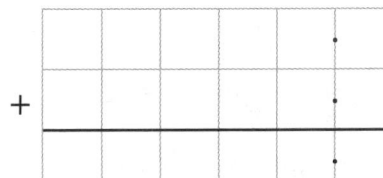

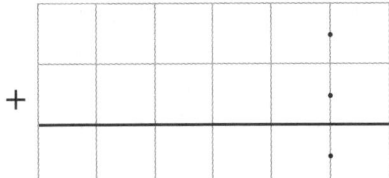

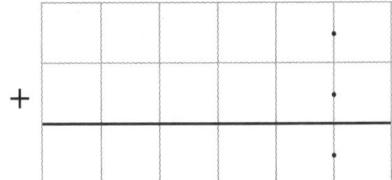

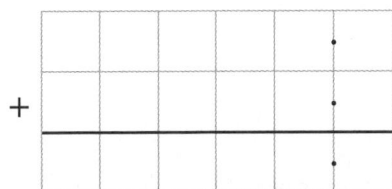

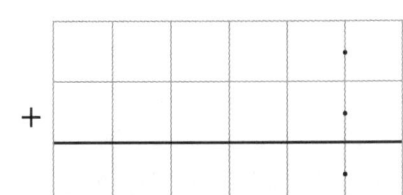

Name: _____ Date: _____

Book sales

- Solve multi-step problems in contexts, deciding which operations and methods to use and why
- Use estimation to check accuracy of answers

The table below shows part of the chart of the top 100 best-selling books of all time.

Position	Type of book	Sales	Rounded to the nearest 1000	Sales increased by 20 000
90th	science	816 907	817 000	836 907
91st	comic annual	816 585		
92nd	novel	815 586		
93rd	novel	814 370		
94th	novel	809 641		
95th	novel	807 311		
96th	novel	806 538		
97th	cookery	794 201		
98th	novel	792 187		
99th	autobiography	791 507		
100th	cookery	791 095		

a Round all the sales to the nearest 1000 and write them in the 4th column.

b If all the books increased their sales by 20 000, what would be the new sales figures? Write these in the last column.

c Use the rounded sales numbers to give an approximation of the total number of cookery books sold. ☐

d Use the rounded sales numbers to work out the difference between the most and least popular book type in the chart. ☐

e The author of the autobiography gave 40 000 copies of his book away for free as he was so proud of it. How many books were paid for?
☐

Name: _____ **Date:** _____

000-in-a-row

Identify the value of each digit in a number with 3 decimal places

You will need:
- 2 different coloured pencils
- 3 × 0–9 dice

Play this game with a partner.

- Take turns to roll the dice.

- Use the digits rolled to make a number less than 1 with 3 decimal places, for example, 0·438.

- Mark your number on the number line, in the approximate place, using your coloured pencil.

- The first player to get three of their numbers in a row is the winner.

Play three games.

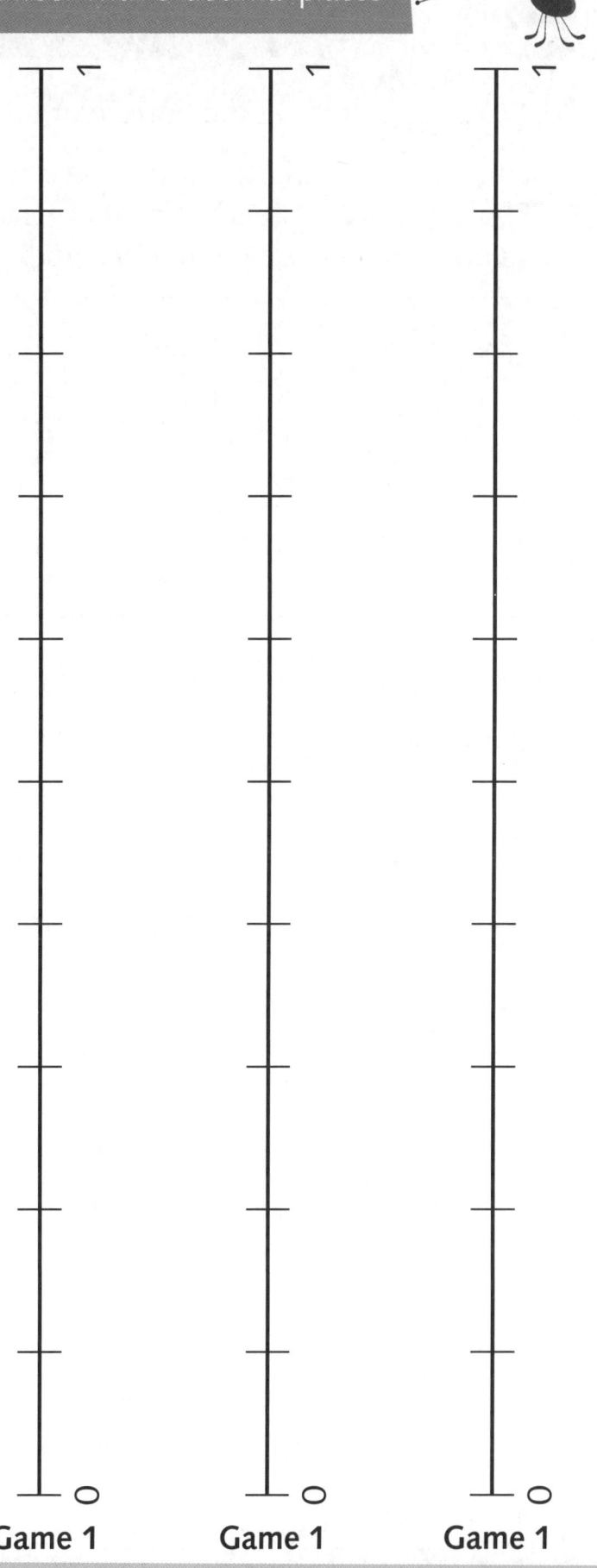

Game 1   Game 1   Game 1

Name: _____ Date: _____

Move the digits

Multiply and divide numbers by 10, 100 and 1000 where the answers are up to 3 decimal places

You will need:
• scissors

- Cut out the cards at the bottom of this sheet.

- Use the cards and the place value chart to help answer these calculations. Place the cards for each 2-digit or decimal number in the correct place value column and then multiply or divide the number by 10, 100 or 1000.

Thousands	Hundreds	Tens	Ones	tenths	hundredths

a $74 \times 100 =$ ☐   d $14 \times 100 =$ ☐   g $2.7 \times 10 =$ ☐

   $74 \div 100 =$ ☐ $14 \div 100 =$ ☐ $2.7 \div 10 =$ ☐

b $2.9 \times 100 =$ ☐   e $0.8 \times 1000 =$ ☐   h $0.96 \times 100 =$ ☐

   $29 \div 10 =$ ☐ $83 \div 100 =$ ☐ $96 \div 100 =$ ☐

c $0.35 \times 100 =$ ☐   f $0.54 \times 10 =$ ☐   i $0.48 \times 1000 =$ ☐

   $35 \div 10 =$ ☐ $54 \div 10 =$ ☐ $48 \div 100 =$ ☐

1	2	3	4	5	6
7	8	9	0	0	0

Name: _____ Date: _____

What other calculations?

Multiply decimals by whole numbers

What multiplication calculations involving decimals will the calculation in the circle help you to work out? Write six different related calculations for each.

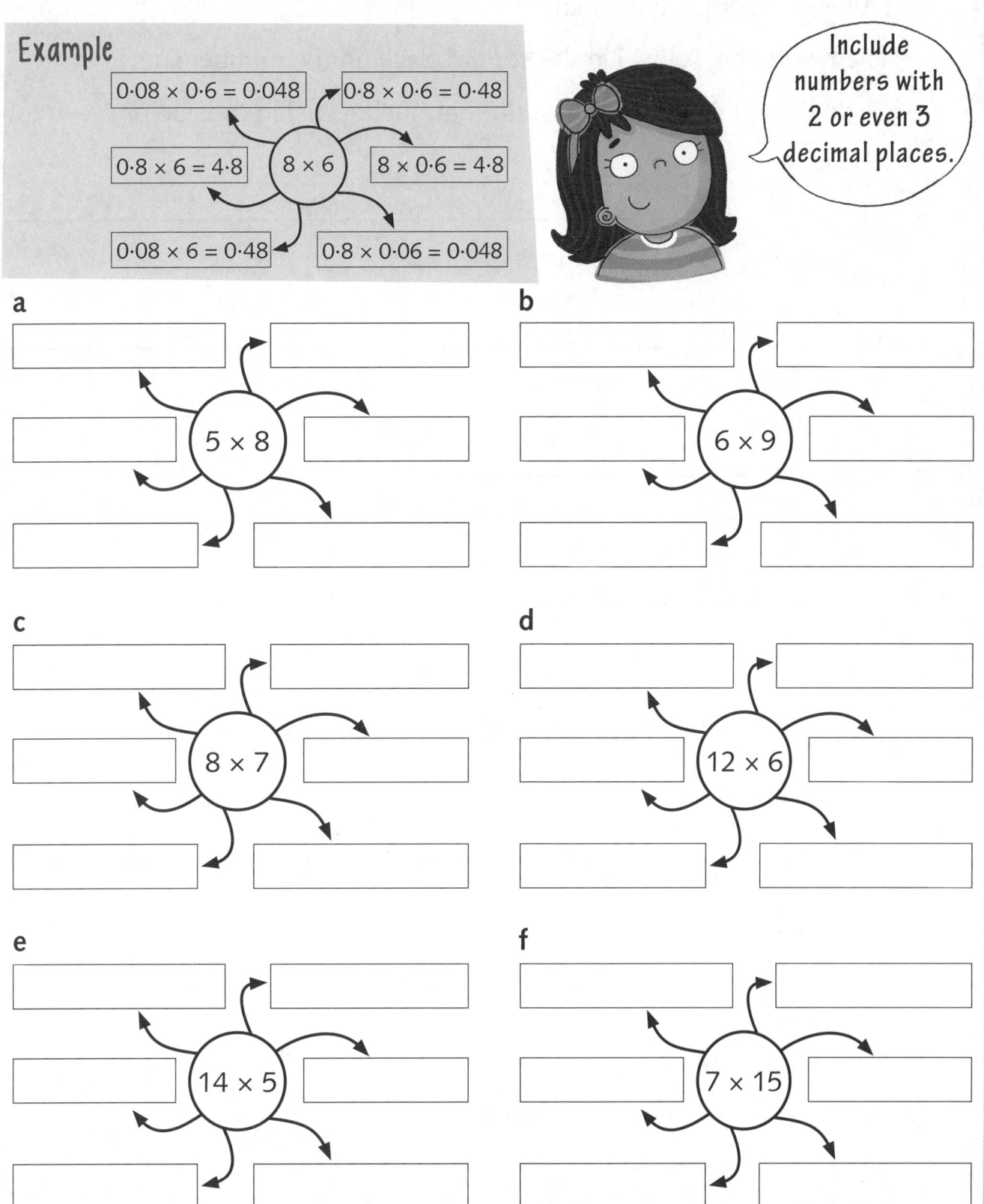

Example

$0.08 \times 0.6 = 0.048$ $0.8 \times 0.6 = 0.48$

$0.8 \times 6 = 4.8$ 8×6 $8 \times 0.6 = 4.8$

$0.08 \times 6 = 0.48$ $0.8 \times 0.06 = 0.048$

Include numbers with 2 or even 3 decimal places.

a 5×8

b 6×9

c 8×7

d 12×6

e 14×5

f 7×15

Name: _____ Date: _____

Rounding up or down?

Round numbers to specified degrees of accuracy

- Write the whole numbers or tenth that each decimal comes between at either end of the number line.

- Then write the decimal in the correct place on the number line.

- Circle the whole number or tenth that the decimal rounds up or down to.

a 4·6

b 2·3

c 7·5

d 9·4

e 1·37

f 5·23

g 3·21

h 6·18

Name: _____ Date: _____

See-saw lengths

Convert from smaller to larger units of length using decimal notation

You will need:
• ruler

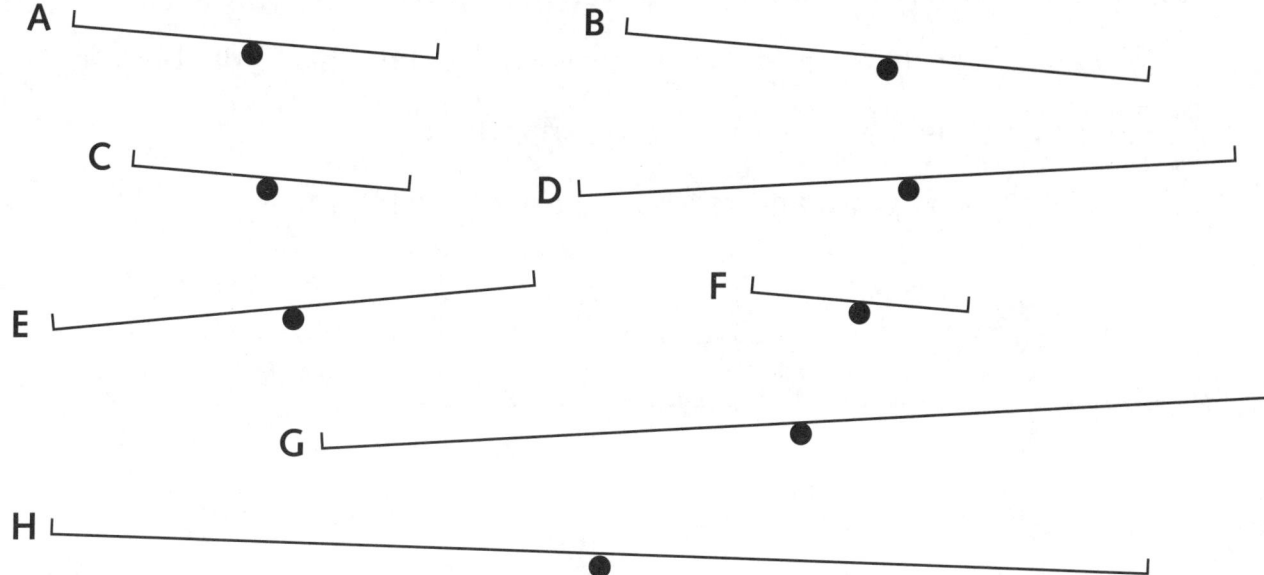

1 Use your ruler to measure the length of each see-saw to the nearest millimetre and record your values in the table below.

2 Calculate the distance from one end of the see-saw to the midpoint of the see-saw. Write your answer in millimetres, then in centimetres and complete the table.

The first one has been done for you.

See-saw	Total length (mm)	Length to midpoint (mm)	Length to midpoint (cm)
A	50	50 ÷ 2 = 25	2·5
B			
C			
D			
E			
F			
G			
H			

Name: _____ Date: _____

Gerry's jumping bean

Convert between units of length to solve problems
using decimal notation

Gerry had a jumping bean.

He placed it over the 4 cm mark on a measuring tape and called that point A.

As soon as he released the bean, it began to jump.

Gerry drew this diagram and recorded how his bean jumped.

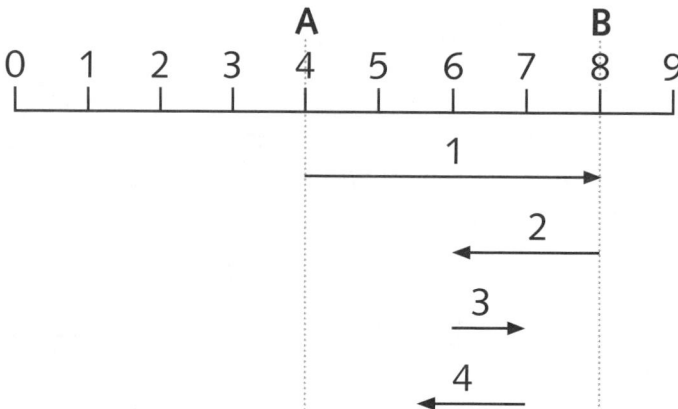

Jump 1:   The bean jumped to point B landing at 8 cm.

Jump 2:   It jumped halfway back to A, landing at 6 cm.

Jump 3:   The bean jumped halfway towards B landing at 7 cm.

Jump 4:   The bean jumped halfway back to A landing at 5·5 cm.

1 Work out the position on the measuring tape where
   Gerry's bean landed after a halfway jump towards B
   and then a halfway jump back to A where it stopped.

2 How far, in millimetres, did the bean jump altogether?

3 Rule a number line from 0 to 10 centimetres on the back of this sheet.
   Mark the intervals for each centimetre. Choose a different starting point
   for your jumping bean.

   a Work out where your bean will finish after a
      total of six halfway forward and backward jumps.

   b Work out how far, in millimetres, your bean jumped.

Name: _____ Date: _____

Motor boat hires

Convert between miles and kilometres

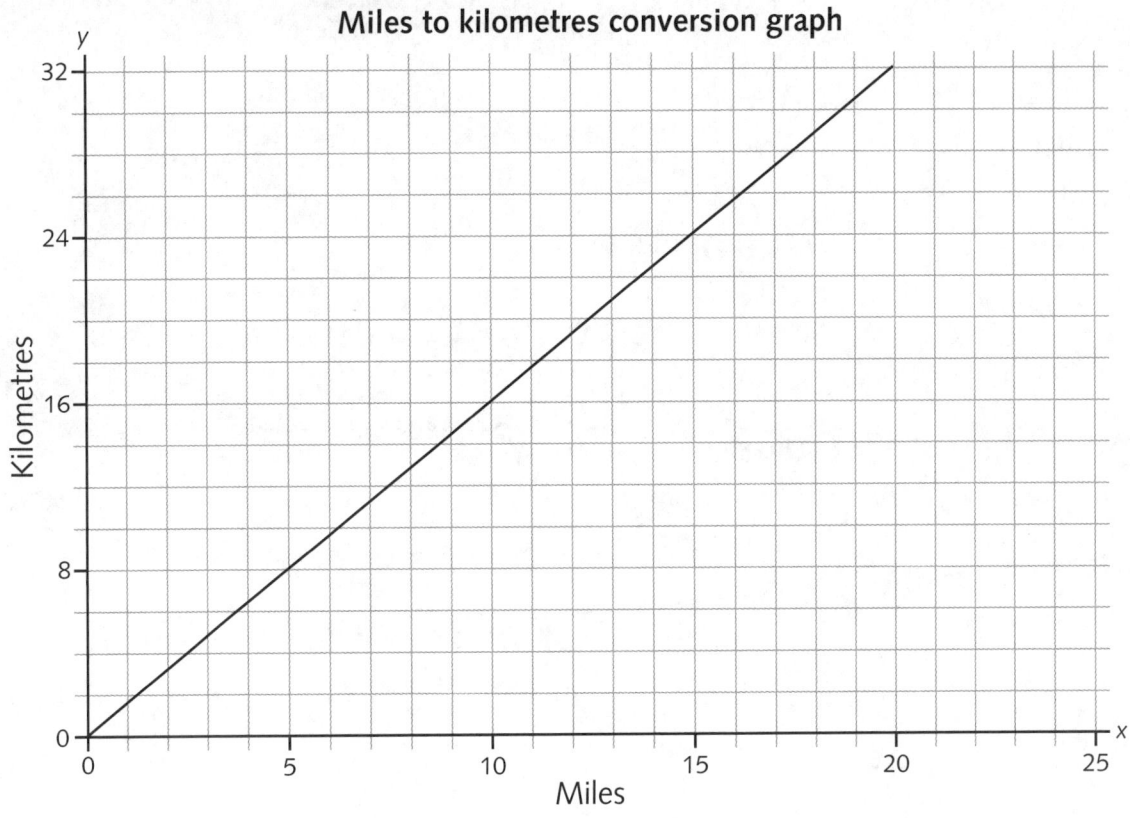

Miles to kilometres conversion graph

Martin hires out motor boats by the day. The table shows the distance each motor boat travelled when hired for one day.

1 Use the graph to convert the distances and complete the table.

2 Write the total distance in miles for the Puffin and Sandpiper.

☐ miles

3 Write the total distance in kilometres for the Tern and the Petrel.

☐ km

Motor boat	Distance (miles)	Distance (km)
Seagull		16
Tern	5	
Puffin		24
Sandpiper	12·5	
Kittiwake	7·5	
Petrel		32
Mallard	17·5	
Guillemot		4

Name: _____ Date: _____

Distances by air

Convert between miles and kilometres

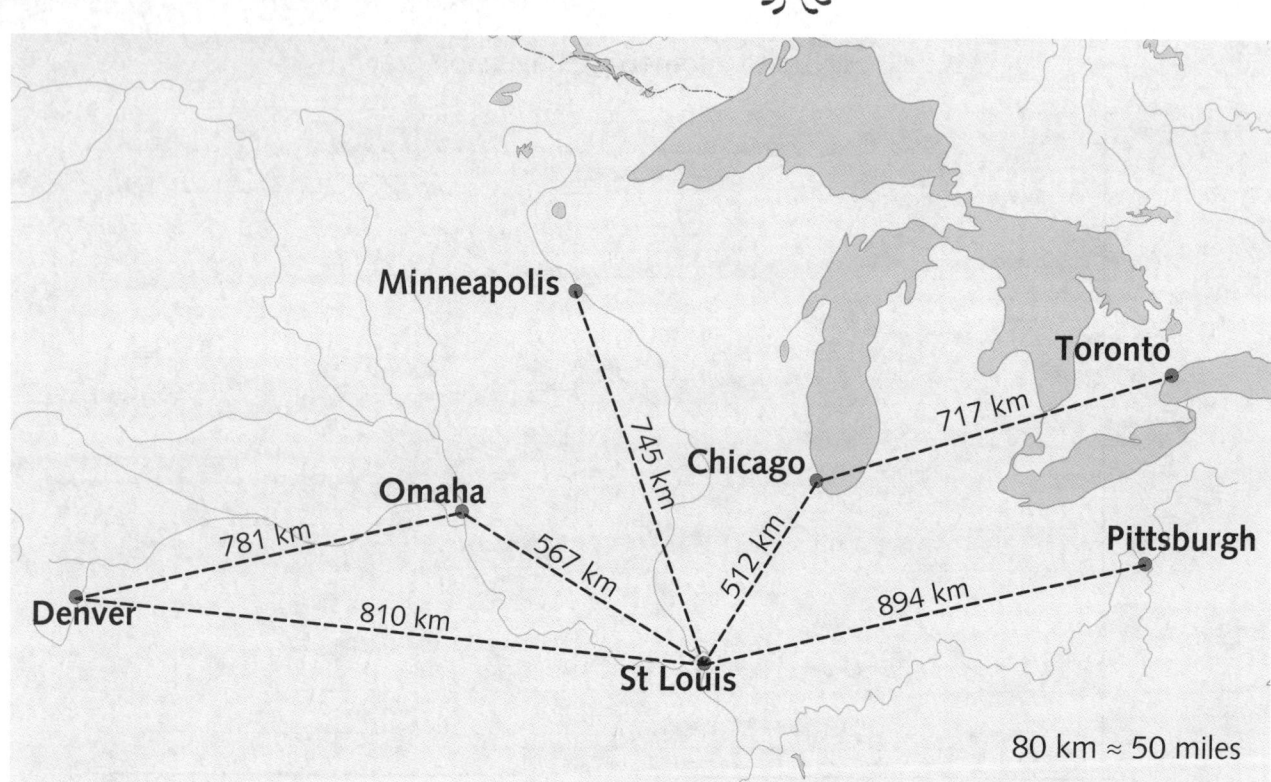

Minneapolis
Toronto
717 km
745 km
Chicago
Omaha
781 km
567 km
512 km
Pittsburgh
Denver
810 km
894 km
St Louis

80 km ≈ 50 miles

1 Use the map to find how many kilometres you would fly on each of these trips.

    a Toronto → Chicago → St Louis   ☐ km

    b Denver → Omaha → St Louis   ☐ km

    c Minneapolis → St Louis → Pittsburgh   ☐ km

    d Denver → St Louis → Chicago → Toronto   ☐ km

2 Convert each distance flown in Question 1 to miles.

    a ☐ miles   **b** ☐ miles

    c ☐ miles   **d** ☐ miles

Name: _____ Date: _____

Multiples and factors

Identify factors and common factors

1 Draw three different factor trees for 36.

2 Write the factors for each pair or trios of numbers, then circle all the common factors.

a 24
36
_____
_____

b 20
30
_____
_____

c 16
40
_____
_____

d 25
50
100
_____
_____
_____

e 32
48
60
_____
_____
_____

Name: _____ Date: _____

Multiples and factors

Identify common factors, common multiples and prime numbers

1 Work out the answer to these problems about factors and multiples.

a All the common factors of 75 and 100 except one are multiples of the same number. What is the number?

b If 3 is not a common factor of a pair of numbers, what other numbers cannot be common factors? Explain your reasons giving examples.

c Some even numbers have only even factors except for 2. Others have odd factors also. Find five examples of each type. Write what you notice.

Example

16 → 1, 2, 4, 8, 16
10 → 1, 2, 5, 10

d Find three pairs of numbers where the second one is double the first one and has twice as many factors as the first one.

e Ben and Harry both play tennis. Ben plays every three days and Harry plays every five days. If they both played on Monday, 1st January, what other dates in January will they both play on the same day? Show your working out and answer on the back of this sheet.

Name: _____ Date: _____

Dividing ThHTO by 11 and 12 using the formal written method of short division

- Use the formal written method to calculate ThHTO ÷ TO
- Estimate and check the answer to a calculation

For each division calculation, write your estimate, then use the formal written method of short division to work out the answer.

Example

$7692 \div 12 \rightarrow$ $7700 \div 10 = 770$

Th	H	T	O
	6	4	1

12	7	6	^{4}9	^{1}2

a $2376 \div 12 \rightarrow$

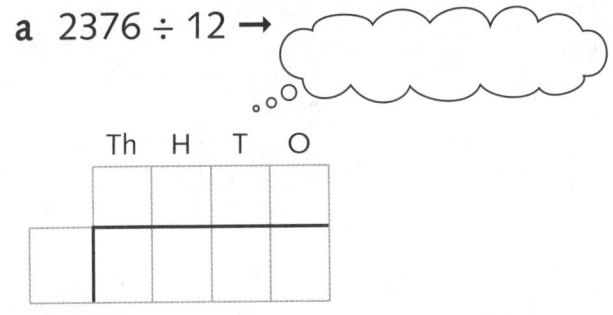

b $2388 \div 12 \rightarrow$

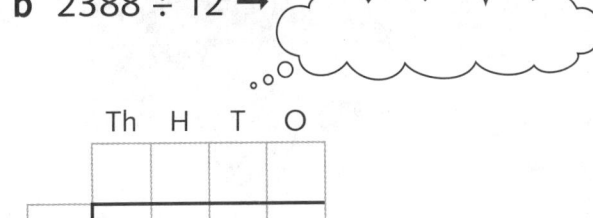

c $3756 \div 12 \rightarrow$

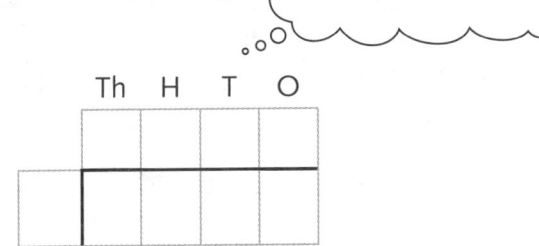

d $4521 \div 11 \rightarrow$

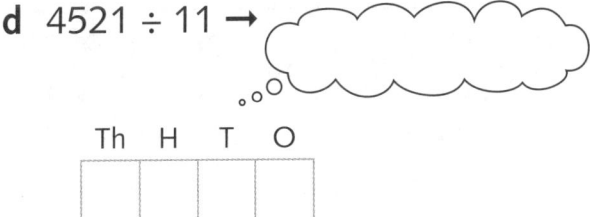

e $2156 \div 11 \rightarrow$

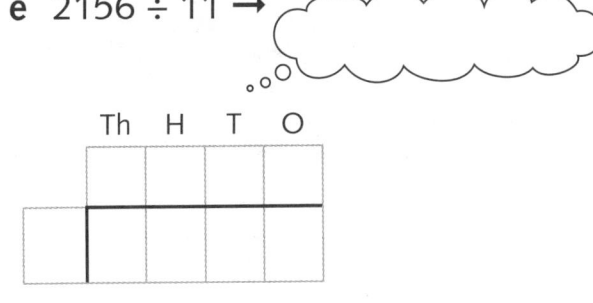

f $4716 \div 12 \rightarrow$

g $3410 \div 11 \rightarrow$

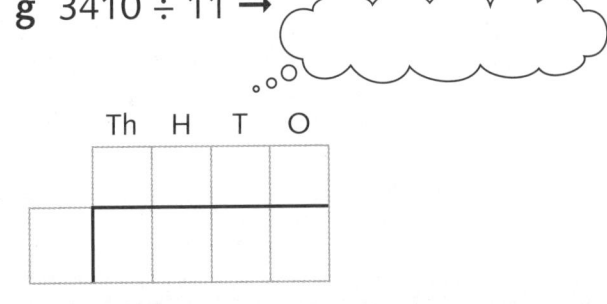

h $5676 \div 11 \rightarrow$

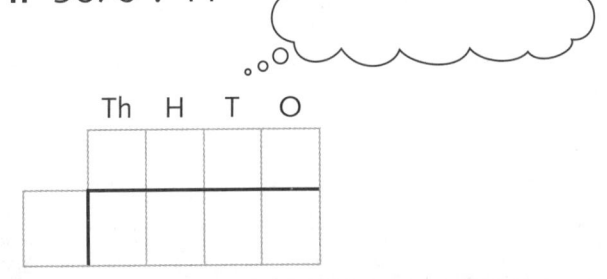

Name: _____ Date: _____

Dividing ThHTO by 11 and 12 using the formal written method of short division

Use the most efficient method to calculate ThHTO ÷ TO

Find the answer to these problems. Show all your working out.

a A florist sells roses by the dozen. At the end of the week, 6816 roses have been sold. How many dozen roses is this?

b One dozen roses cost £24. The florist sells £3456 worth of roses in a week. How many roses is this in total?

c Tulips are sold in bunches of 11. At the end of the week, 7579 tulips have been sold. How many bunches is this?

d Tulips cost £11 per bunch. Lilies cost £12 per bunch. The shop takes £1166 on tulips and £1896 on lilies. How many bunches of flowers did it sell in total?

e The answer is £413.75. What could the question be?

_____

_____

_____

f On the back of this sheet write your own word problem involving dividing by 11 or 12 for a friend to solve. Don't make it too easy!

Name: _____ Date: _____

raction and decimal triangles

Associate a fraction with division and calculate decimal fraction equivalents

You will need:
- scissors

Where two triangles are touching, write a fraction on one side of the line, then write its equivalent decimal on the other. You could also use fraction and decimal addition or subtraction calculations.

1 Complete this triangle diagram with equivalent decimals and fractions.

2 Now cut out all the triangles. Shuffle them and give them to a partner to put back together.

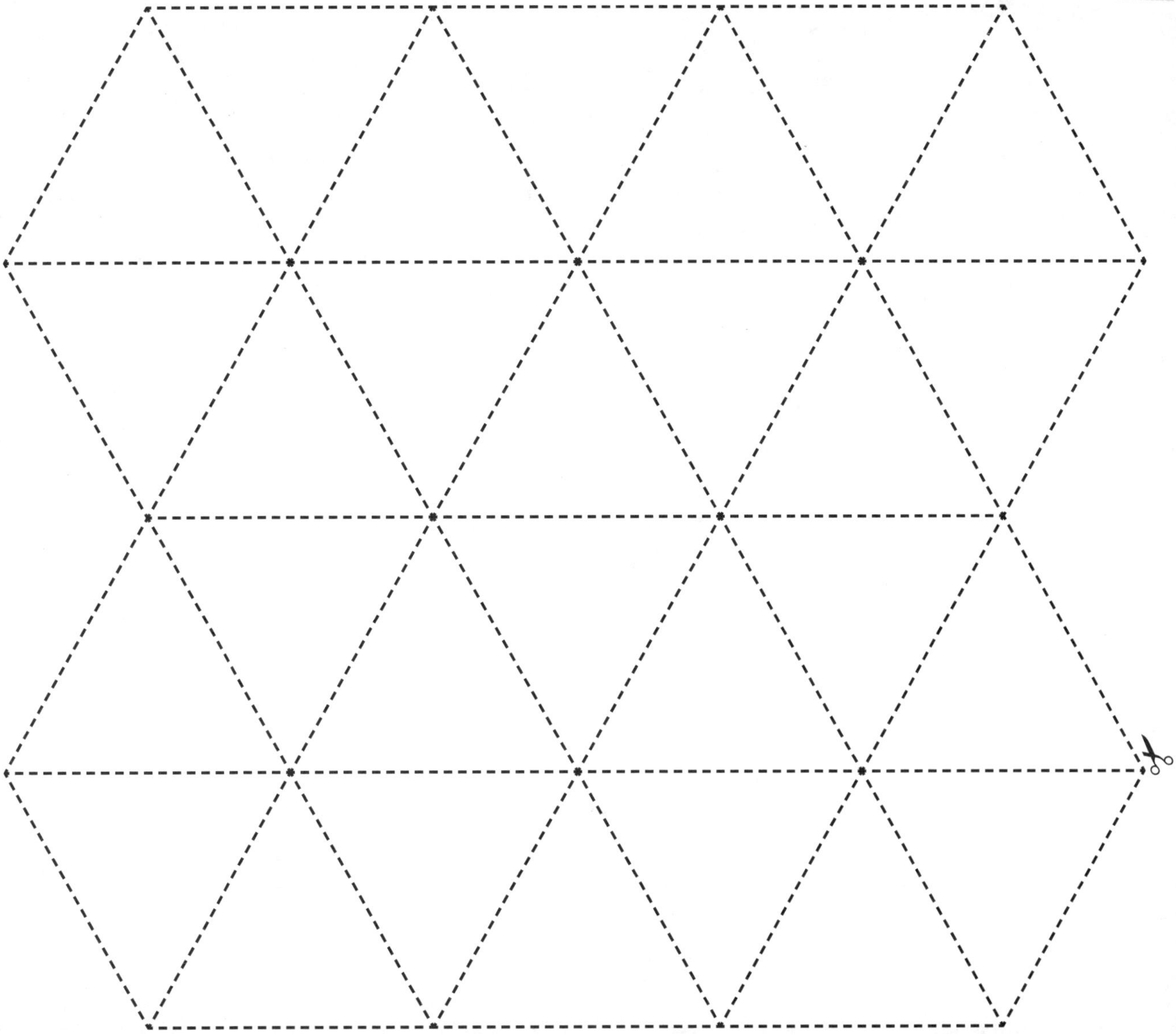

Example

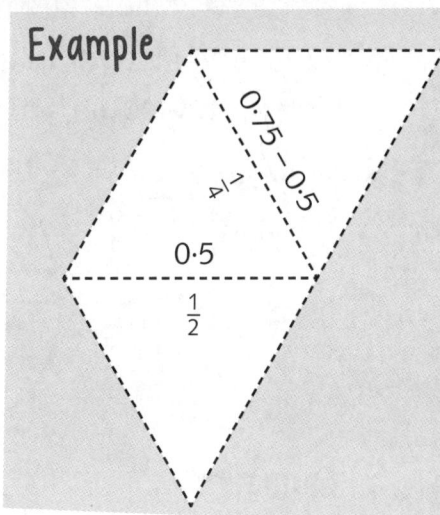

Name: _____ Date: _____

One divided

Associate a fraction with division and calculate decimal fraction equivalents

- Work out each division calculation to convert the fraction to a decimal.
- Write the answer in each segment of the circle, then add up the segments to check they equal one whole.

a Halves

$1 \div 2 =$ [ ]

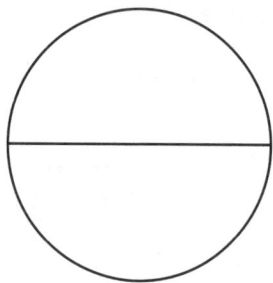

Checking calculation

b Quarters

$1 \div 4 =$ [ ]

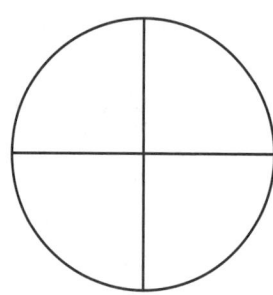

Checking calculation

c Fifths

$1 \div 5 =$ [ ]

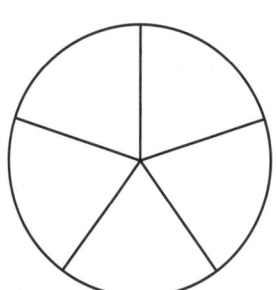

Checking calculation

d Tenths

$1 \div 10 =$ [ ]

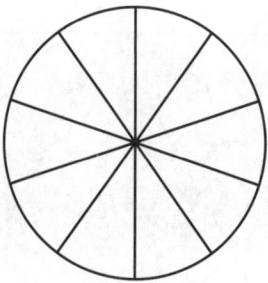

Checking calculation

e Eighths

$1 \div 8 =$ [ ]

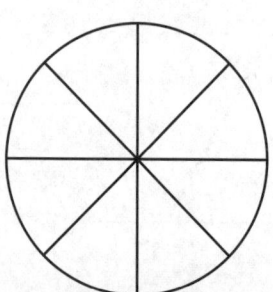

Checking calculation

Name: _____ Date: _____

-in-a-row

Recall and use equivalences between fractions, decimals and percentages

Play this game with a partner.

This game is like noughts and crosses, except each player chooses a different fraction, decimal or percentage to play with.

The aim is to get three equivalent fractions, decimals or percentages in a row.

The winner is the player who writes the fraction, decimal or percentage that completes the row.

I can win now as there is a place where I can write something equivalent to 0·6!

Example

0·1		$\frac{3}{5}$
	60%	
10%	$\frac{1}{10}$	0·6

Name: _____ Date: _____

Theatre percentages

Solve problems involving the calculation of percentages
and the use of percentages for comparison

You will need:
• four coloured
  pencils

- Use the grids to represent the problems below.

- Use a different coloured pencil for each percentage.

- Fill in the missing percentages.

a 25% of people arrived by bus.
35% of people arrived on foot.
30% of people arrived by train.

[ ] % of people arrived by car.

b 40% of people ate chocolate ice cream.
15% of people ate butterscotch ice cream.
23% of people ate strawberry ice cream.

[ ] % of people ate vanilla ice cream.

c 34% of people had expensive seats.
47% of people had standard seats.
10% of people had cheap seats.

[ ] % of people had very expensive seats.

d 65% of people really enjoyed the play.
21% of people enjoyed it.
13% of people were not sure.

[ ] % of people did not enjoy it.

Name: _____ Date: _____

ime dominoes

Convert from smaller to larger units of time and vice versa

You will need:
• scissors

Play this game with a partner.
- Cut out the domino cards, shuffle them and take six cards each.
- Start with any domino.
- Take turns to join a matching domino to one of the ends.
  If you can't go, you miss a turn.

The winner is the first player to use up all of their dominoes.

4 min 10 s	2 days
2 min 15 s	2 weeks
10 min	180 min
5 min	110 min
125 s	600 min
200 s	165 min

48 hours	135 s
14 days	600 s
3 hours	300 s
1 h 50 min	2 min 5 s
10 hours	3 min 20 s
2 h 45 min	250 s

Name: _____   Date: _____

Domino times

Convert from smaller to larger units of time and vice versa

You will need:
• scissors

Play this game with a partner.
- Cut out the domino cards, shuffle them and take six cards each.
- Start with any domino.
- Take turns to join a matching domino to one of the ends.
  If you can't go, you miss a turn.

The winner is the first player to use up all of their dominoes.

30 months	210 days		30 weeks	$3\frac{1}{2}$ h
210 min	210 s		$3\frac{1}{2}$ min	3 weeks
21 days	2 years 9 months		21 months	129 min
2 h 9 min	2 min 9 s		129 s	150 min
$2\frac{1}{2}$ h	150 s		$2\frac{1}{2}$ min	5 weeks
35 days	120 h		5 days	$2\frac{1}{2}$ years

Name: _____ Date: _____

econdary school visit

Calculate and convert between units of time to solve problems

Tanya is starting secondary school in September.

This is the timetable for her one day induction visit.

Braeside Secondary School
Induction visit timetable

09:00	Registration in hall	
09:10	Lesson 1	**English**
10:00	Lesson 2	**Mathematics**
10:50	Break	
11:10	Lesson 3	**French**
12:00	Lunch	
13:00	Registration in form room	
13:10	Lesson 4	**Science**
14:00	Break	
14:10	Lesson 5	**P.E.**
15:00	End of day	

1 How many minutes long is each lesson?

[   ] min

2 How much time altogether will she spend in lessons?

[   ] h [   ] min

3 How much time will she **not** spend in lessons?

[   ] h [   ] min

4 When she is halfway through Lesson 2, how many minutes is it until:

a morning break? [   ] min

b lunch? [   ] min

c the start of the French lesson? [   ] min

5 The clock in the science room shows 1:47 p.m. [   ]

How many minutes is it until:

a aftenoon break? [   ] min

b Tanya's induction day at Braeside Secondary School is over? [   ] min

Name: _____ Date: _____

Applying units of speed

Calculate and apply speed using compound units

1 Use the average speed and time to work out how far each of the following travelled.

a	swift	500 m/min for 7 minutes	⬜	m
b	caterpillar	20 cm/min for 15 minutes	⬜	cm
c	hare	75 m/min for 4 minutes	⬜	m
d	horse	0·3 km/min for 12 minutes	⬜	km
e	snail	0·6 cm/min for $1\frac{1}{2}$ hours	⬜	cm
f	spider	40 mm/s for $\frac{1}{4}$ minute	⬜	mm
g	ant	1·5 cm/s for $1\frac{1}{2}$ minutes	⬜	cm
h	beetle	0·01 m/s for 2 minutes	⬜	m
i	greyhound	60 km/h for 2 minutes	⬜	km
j	racing pigeon	144 km/h for 5 minutes	⬜	km
k	mouse	2·4 km/h for 1 minute	⬜	m
l	dragonfly	480 m/h for 15 minutes	⬜	m

2 At an average speed of 15 m per minute, how many metres can a Texas cowboy drive his cattle in 2 hours? ⬜ m

3 A migrating bird flies at an average speed of 0·4 km per minute. How many kilometres will it fly in 12 hours? ⬜ km

4 Using the information in Question 1, write one question for a friend to answer. Record your answer on the back of this sheet.

_____

_____

_____

Name: _____ Date: _____

Negative tug of war

Use negative numbers and calculate intervals across 0

Play this game with a partner.

You will need:
- 0–9 dice
- counter

- Decide who will be positivenumbers and who will be negative numbers.

- Put the counter on zero on the number line.

- Take turns to roll the dice.

- The positive player moves the counter to the right.The negative player moves the counter to the left.

- Use the dice at the bottom of the sheet to keep track of your goes.

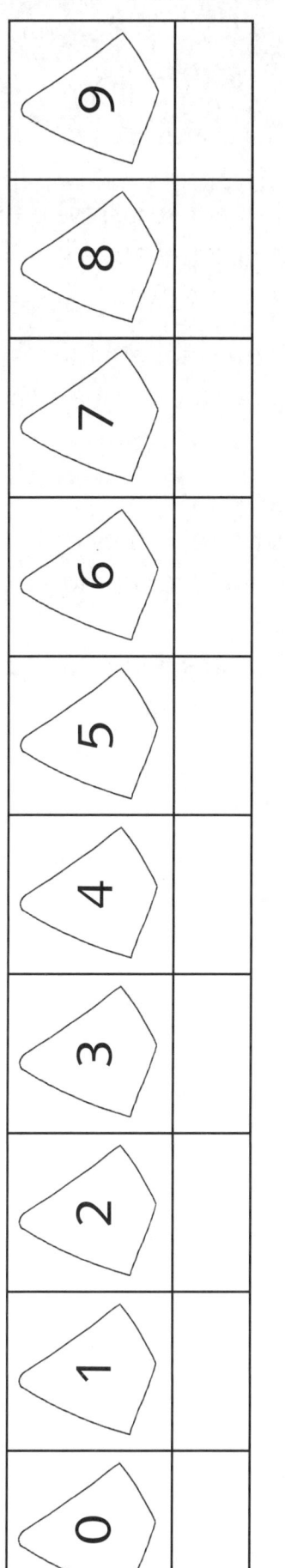

Name: _____ Date: _____

4-in-a-row

Use negative numbers in context

- Design a 4-in-a-row game involving negative numbers on the grid below.

- Use the spinners for players to generate numbers to cover on the grid.

Points to consider:
  - What numbers do you want to include on the grid?
  - How will the numbers on the spinners relate to the numbers on the grid?

Hint
Remember that in a game of 4-in-a-row, the winner is the first player to connect four numbers in a row column or diagonal.

Name: _____ Date: _____

rackets first!

Use knowledge of the order of operations to carry out calculations involving the four operations

Work out these calculations using the BODMAS rule.

The part of the calculation that must be worked out first is in **bold**.

a **(20 + 12)** × 3 ☐ × 3 =	**b** **(7 + 18)** × 4 ☐ × 4 =	**c** **(25 – 9)** × 5 ☐ × 5 =
d **(12 – 8)** × 11 ☐ × 11 =	**e** 20 × **(8 – 4)** ☐ × 20 =	**f** 6 × **(3 + 5)** 6 × ☐ =
g 3 × **(3 + 2 + 3)** 3 × ☐ =	**h** **(18 + 12)** × 6 ☐ × 6 =	**i** **(24 – 12)** × 2 ☐ × 2 =
j **(2 + 7)** × **(1 + 3)** ☐ × ☐ =	**k** **(3 × 3)** – **(2 × 2)** ☐ – ☐ =	**l** **(21 + 3)** × **(18 + 4)** ☐ × ☐ =

Name: _____ Date: _____

3-angle puzzle

Identify angles at a point and one whole turn (total 360°)

A game for two or three players.

You will need:
• scissors

• Cut out the cards below. Shuffle them and place them face down in rows on the table.

• Take turns to turn over three cards. If the sum of their angles is 360°, take the cards and continue with your turn.

• If the sum of their angles is not 360°, turn the cards face down again. Play passes to the next player.

The winner is the player with the most cards. There will be three cards left when all possible sets of three have been made.

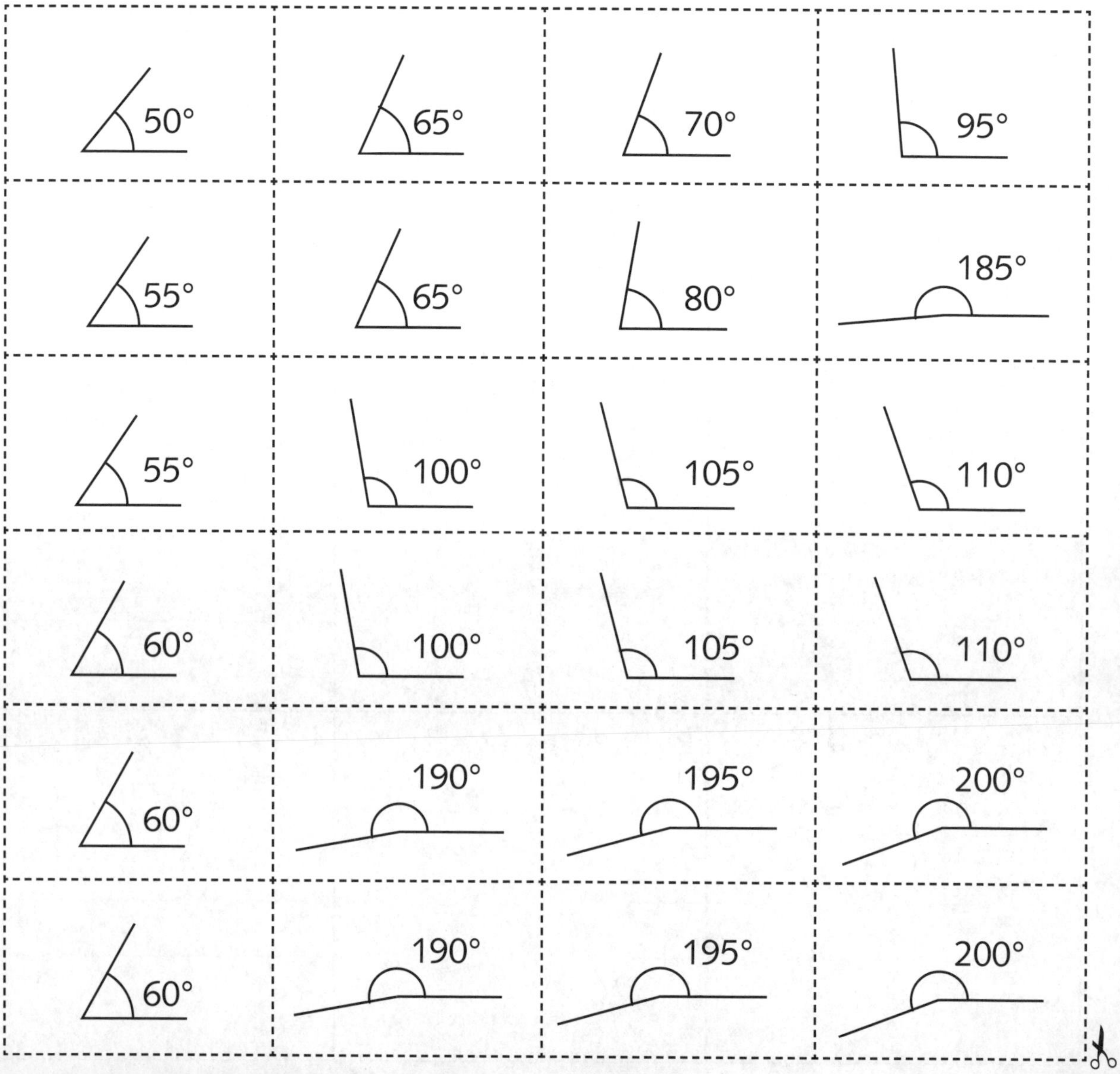

50°	65°	70°	95°
55°	65°	80°	185°
55°	100°	105°	110°
60°	100°	105°	110°
60°	190°	195°	200°
60°	190°	195°	200°

Name: _____ Date: _____

oll the dice

- Add whole numbers using the formal written methods
- Estimate the answer to a calculation

You will need:
- 0–9 dice

Play this game on your own or with a partner.

- Roll the dice 13 times.
- After each roll fill in one of the spaces on a calculation grid.
- When all 13 spaces are full, add up the numbers.
- Try to get an answer as close to 5 000 000 as you can. If you are playing with a partner, the person with the closest number scores 1 point. The overall winner is the player with the most points after four rounds. If it's a draw, use the back of this sheet to play a fifth round.

Name: _____ Date: _____

Simplifying and using formulae games

Use simple formulae

> **Remember**
> in algebra 2 × a is written as 2a. The × sign is missed out.

You will need:
• scissors
• 1–6 dice

Play this game with a partner

Game 1

• Cut out the 24 cards at the bottom of the sheet. There are 12 matching pairs.
• Place the cards face down in rows on the table. Take turns to turn over two cards.
• If your cards match, you win the pair and have another go. If they don't match, put them back.

The winner is the player with the most cards once all the cards have been paired.

Game 2

• Roll the dice three times to find values for a, b and c. Fill in the table.

$a =$	$b =$	$c =$

• Shuffle the cards and deal them out so that you have 12 cards each.
• Each work through the calculations for your own cards, and check each other's calculations.
• Who has the card with the highest value? It might be a draw.

5a	3b + 6b	3 × b	6b
6c − 4c	5 × a	7b − b	4b
3b	2 × a	c	15c − 14c
a + a + a	7c	10c	8a + 2a
10 × c	8b − 4b	2c + 3c + 2c	2c
2a	3a	9b	10a

Name: _____ Date: _____

Investigating triangular numbers

- Generate and describe linear number sequences
- Use simple formulae

These numbers are called 'triangular numbers', because they can form a triangle.

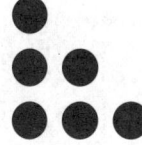

1   1 + 2 = 3   1 + 2 + 3 = 6

1 Draw and write a calculation for the next five triangular numbers then fill in the table.

Working out

	1st	2nd	3rd	4th	5th	6th	7th	8th
Triangular number	1	3	6					

2 Answer the following questions about triangular numbers. Show your working out and answers on the back of this sheet.

a Look at the differences between consecutive terms. What do you notice?

b Try mentally adding pairs of consecutive triangular numbers.
   - What do you notice about the answers?
   - Do you think that they will always be this special type of number?
   - Can you explain why?

c Work out the formula for the nth triangular number. Share your ideas with a partner.

> **Hint**
> Think about putting consecutive triangular numbers together.

Name: _____ Date: _____

Lucky numbers

- Express missing number problems algebraically
- Use simple formulae

Some people say that their lucky number is 7. But Constance, Anna, Ben and Sajid, all say that 7 is not their lucky number. Constance says, 'If you multiply my lucky number by 4 and take away 2, it makes 10'. Her friends write an algebraic equation for her lucky number: $4x - 2 = 10$. They solve the equation to find her lucky number: $4x = 12$, so her lucky number is 3 .

Read what each child says, and use the information to write an equation. Then solve the equation to find the lucky numbers in a similar way.

1 Anna says, "If you add 5 to my number and divide by 2, it makes 7."

Working out

2 Ben says, "If you find the square of my number and add 3, it makes 7."

Working out

3 Sajid says, "If you multiply my lucky number by 5 and then take away 13, you are left with 7."

Working out

4 On the back of this sheet, write a sentence and an equation for your lucky 1-digit number for a friend to solve. If your lucky number has already been chosen, write one for a number that has not been chosen yet.

Name: _____ Date: _____

esigning a patio

- Find pairs of numbers that satisfy an equation with two unknowns
- List possible combinations of two variables

A builder has bought 504 square patio slabs at a bargain price. There are no more available.

He wants to make a rectangular patio using all the slabs.

Hint
Total number of slabs in patio N = number of slabs in length (l) × number of slabs in width (w)

There are 12 different ways of laying the slabs, although some might make some unusual shaped patios. How many can you find?

Working out

Name: _____ Date: _____

5-piece puzzle

Draw 2-D shapes accurately and use conventional markings for lines and angles

You will need:
• protractor
• ruler
• scissors

1 a Use your protractor and ruler to construct the square on the right in the space below.

b Cut out the five shapes.

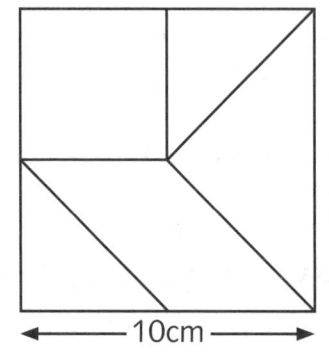

— 10cm —

Hint
This square is not drawn to scale!

2 Use all five shapes to make this hexagon.

3 On the hexagon, use symbols to:

• label each pair of equal sides
• label each pair of parallel sides
• label each pair of equal angles.

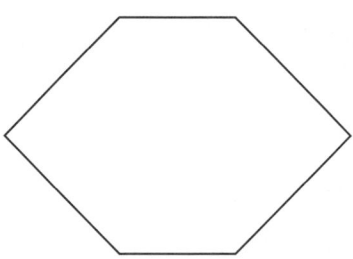

Name: _____ Date: _____

ngles in regular polygons

Use properties to classify 2-D shapes and find the missing angles in 2-D shapes

When you divide a regular polygon into triangles you can calculate the sum of its interior angles.

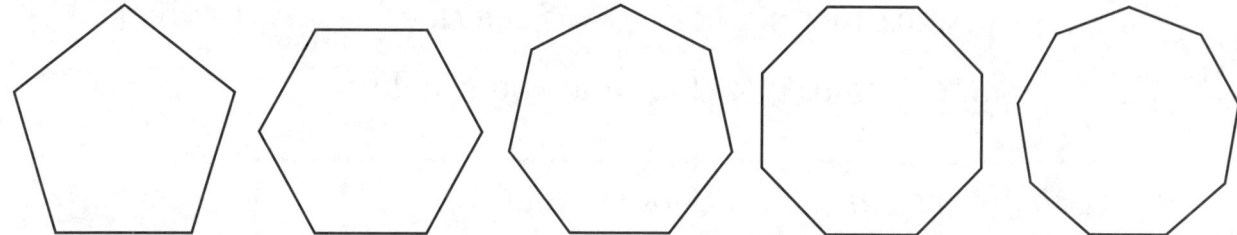

The table below shows the results for an equilateral triangle and a square.

Number of sides	Number of triangles	Sum of interior angles	Size of interior angle
3	1	180° × 1 = 180°	180° ÷ 3 = 60°
4	2	180° × 2 = 360°	360° ÷ 4 = 90°
5	3		
6			
7			
8			
9			

1 Divide each regular polygon into triangles by drawing diagonal lines from one vertex to all the other vertices in the polygon.

2 Complete the table above.

- To find the sum of the interior angles: multiply 180° by the number of triangles.

- To find the size of the interior angle: divide the sum of the interior angles by the number of sides of the polygon.

3 Look for patterns in the table and use them to find the size of the interior angle of a dodecagon.

Sum of interior angles = [ ]°   Size of interior angle = [ ]°

Name: _____ Date: _____

Shapes on a pinboard

Identify and describe the properties of 2-D shapes

A game for two players.

- In pairs, take turns to secretly choose one of the shapes below. On your turn, give your partner no more than three clues to find the shape.

- Here are some examples of clues that you could use:

> *The shape has one pair of parallel sides.*
> *The shape has two acute and two obtuse angles.*
> *The shape is not symmetrical.*
> *The shape has five pins on its perimeter.*

- Your partner must point to and name the shape correctly. The first player to identify five shapes correctly is the winner.

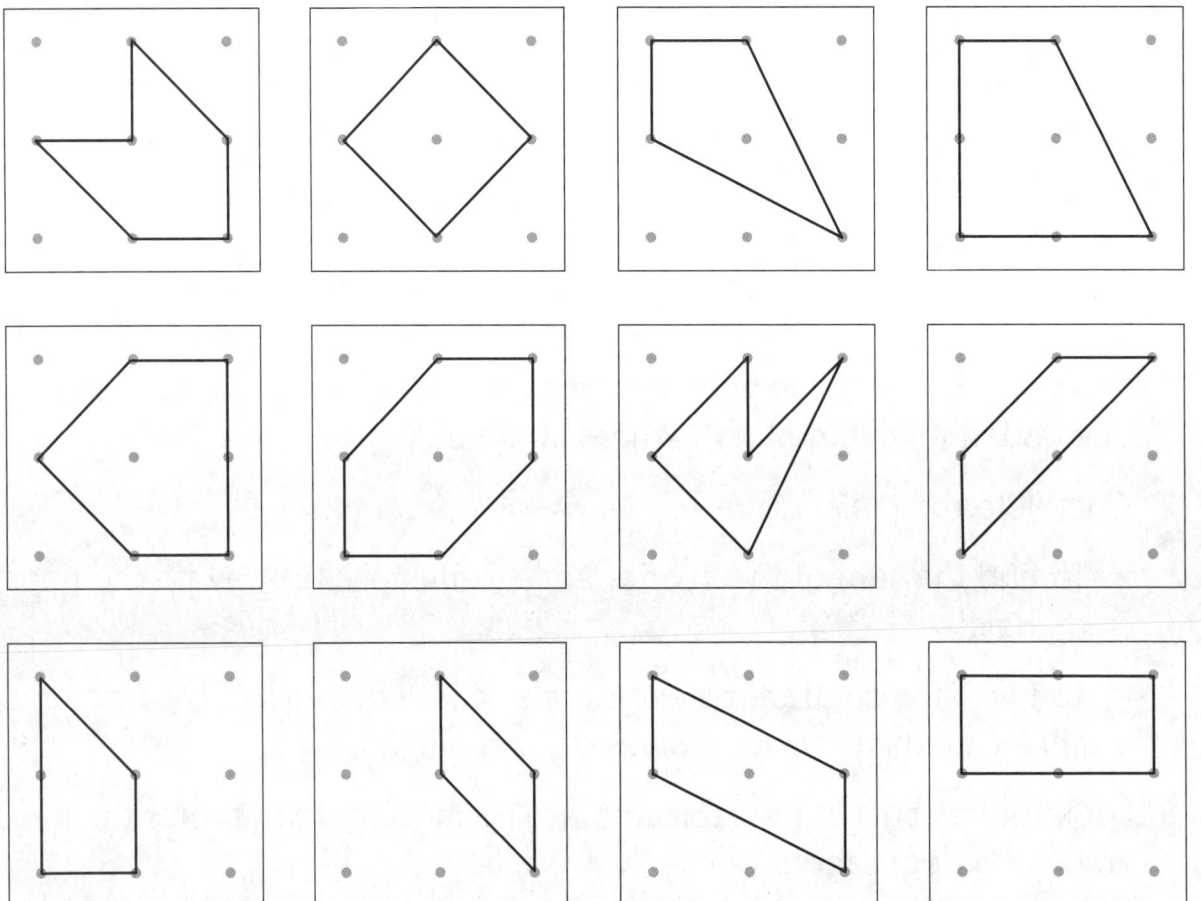

Name: _____ Date: _____

Multiplication HTO x TO using partitioning

- Use partitioning to calculate HTO × TO
- Estimate and check the answer to a calculation

Estimate the answer first, then partition each of these calculations to work out the answer. Check your answer is close to your estimated answer.

Example

$263 \times 38 \rightarrow (300 \times 40 = 12\ 000)$

$= (200 \times 38) + (60 \times 38) + (3 \times 38)$

$= 7600 + 2280 + 114$

$= 9994$

a $354 \times 23 \rightarrow$	**b** $264 \times 25 \rightarrow$
c $482 \times 15 \rightarrow$	**d** $189 \times 32 \rightarrow$
e $574 \times 35 \rightarrow$	**f** $396 \times 44 \rightarrow$
g $472 \times 56 \rightarrow$	**h** $368 \times 29 \rightarrow$

Name: _____ Date: _____

Multiplication HTO x TO using the expanded written method

- Use the expanded written method to calculate HTO × TO
- Estimate and check the answer to a calculation

For each calculation, estimate the answer first, then use the expanded written method to work out the answer. Use your preferred method. Check your answer is close to your estimated answer.

Example

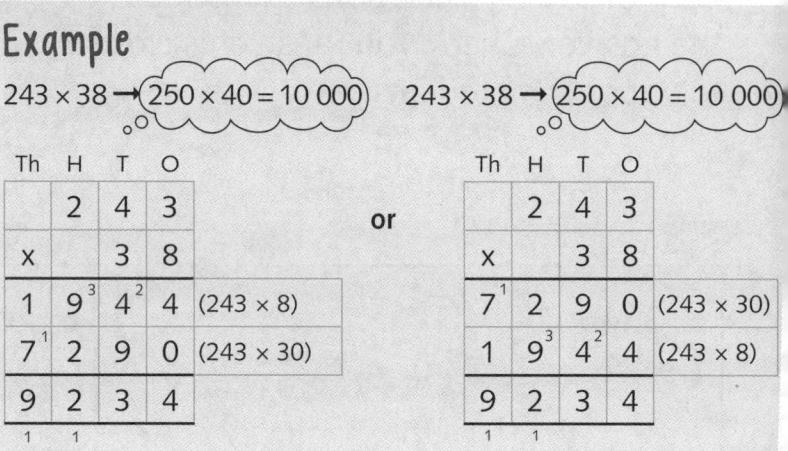

$243 \times 38 \rightarrow 250 \times 40 = 10\,000$

Th	H	T	O	
	2	4	3	
×		3	8	
1	9³	4²	4	(243 × 8)
7¹	2	9	0	(243 × 30)
9	2	3	4	

or

$243 \times 38 \rightarrow 250 \times 40 = 10\,000$

Th	H	T	O	
	2	4	3	
×		3	8	
7¹	2	9	0	(243 × 30)
1	9³	4²	4	(243 × 8)
9	2	3	4	

---

a 263 × 39 →

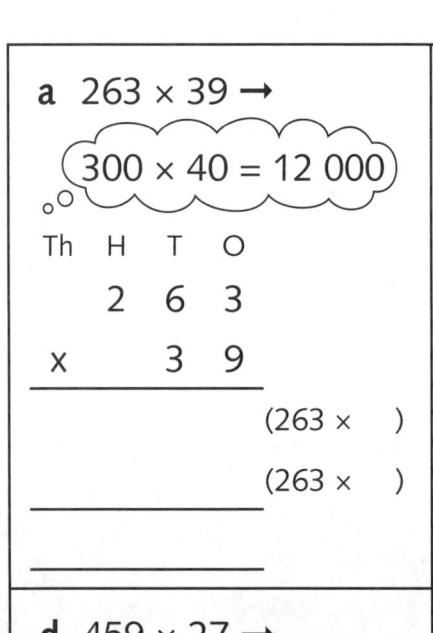

$300 \times 40 = 12\,000$

Th	H	T	O
	2	6	3
×		3	9

(263 ×)

(263 ×)

---

b 354 × 24 →

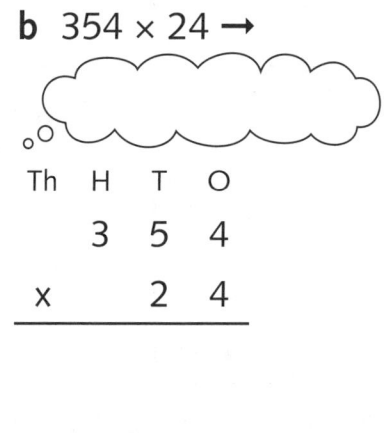

Th	H	T	O
	3	5	4
×		2	4

---

c 286 × 45 →

Th	H	T	O
	2	8	6
×		4	5

---

d 459 × 27 →

Th	H	T	O
	4	5	9
×		2	7

---

e 573 × 36 →

Th	H	T	O
	5	7	3
×		3	6

---

f 465 × 58 →

Th	H	T	O
	4	6	5
×		5	8

Name: _____ Date: _____

ultiplication HTO x TO using the expanded written method

- Use the expanded written method to calculate HTO × TO
- Estimate and check the answer to a calculation

For each pyramid, multiply the numbers next to each other on the bottom row to make the numbers on the next row. Repeat for each row until you reach the total in the star at the top of the pyramid.

a

| 24 | 9 | 3 |
| 8 | 3 | 3 | 1 |

b

| 6 | 4 | 2 | 3 |

c

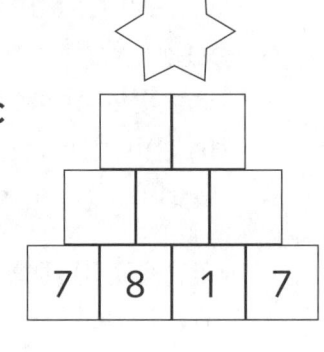

| 7 | 8 | 1 | 7 |

d

| 9 | 4 | 2 | 4 |

e

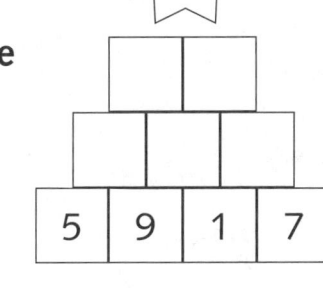

| 5 | 9 | 1 | 7 |

f

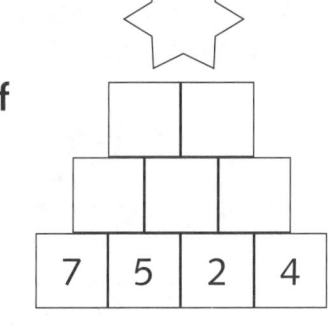

| 7 | 5 | 2 | 4 |

g

| 6 | 9 | 2 | 2 |

h

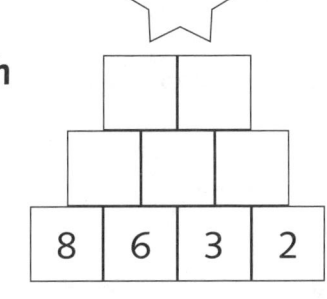

| 8 | 6 | 3 | 2 |

Working out

Name: _____ Date: _____

Multiplication HTO x TO using the formal written method

- Use the formal written method of long multiplication to calculate HTO × TO
- Estimate and check the answer to a calculation

Play this game with a partner.

- Take turns to:
  - choose two numbers from the box
  - write a multiplication calculation
  - estimate the answer, then choose a possible answer from the number board, putting a counter on this number
  - work out the answer using the formal written method.

- If your estimation was correct, leave your counter on the board. If not, remove it from the board.

- Continue until a player has joined three numbers together.

You will need:
- 12 counters each (different colour per person)

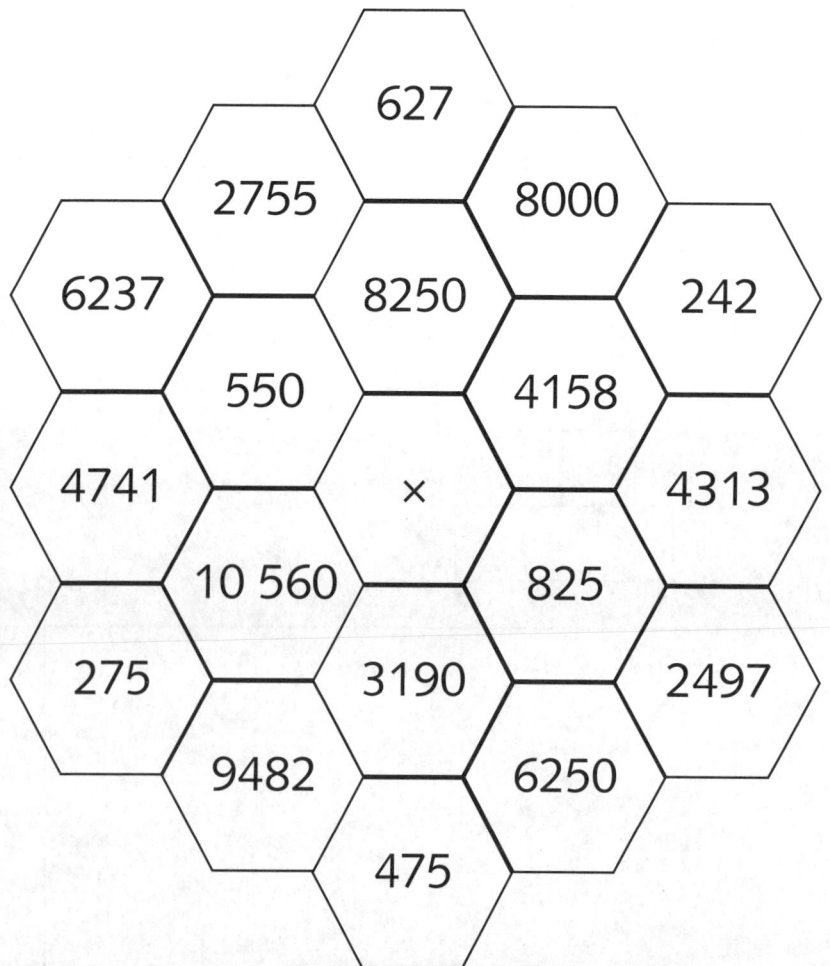

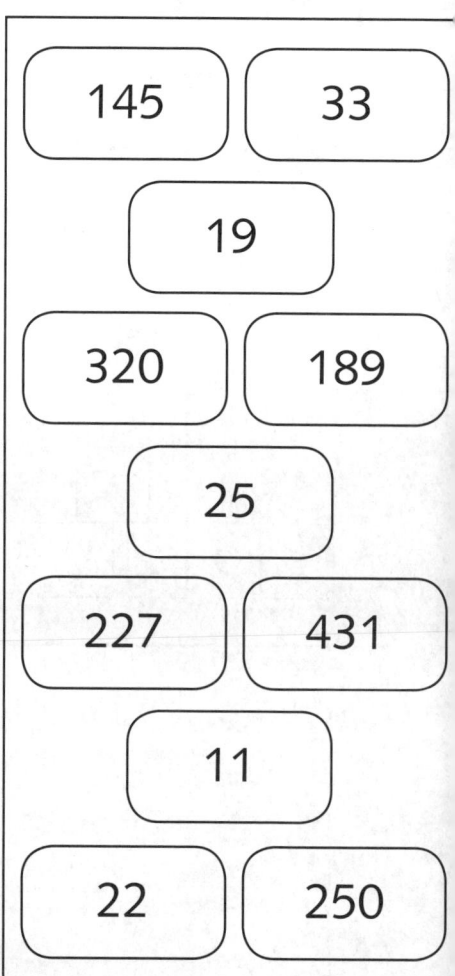

Name: _____ Date: _____

Multiplying decimals using mental methods

Use mental methods to multiply a
decimal by a whole number

You will need:
- scissors
- glue
- sheet of paper

Cut out the multiplication cards.
Arrange them into sets of three
related facts. Then glue the three
facts in each set underneath each
other onto the sheet of paper and
write the answers.

Example
$6 \times 8 = 48$
$0.6 \times 8 = 4.8$
$0.06 \times 8 = 0.48$

0.7×8	0.6×4	7×8	0.09×6	6×4
0.4×9	7×3	0.09×9	0.1×6	0.7×3
5×7	0.6×6	0.06×4	0.04×9	0.06×6
9×9	0.5×8	6×6	0.05×8	4×9
0.9×6	0.01×6	0.07×8	0.07×3	0.5×7
1×6	9×6	5×8	0.9×9	0.05×7

Name: _____   Date: _____

Multiplying decimals using mental methods

Use mental methods to multiply a decimal by a whole number

Work out the answer to each calculation and then write two related facts.

Example

$62 \times 8 =$ ⟨496⟩ $6 \cdot 2 \times 8 = 49 \cdot 6$ $0 \cdot 62 \times 8 = 4 \cdot 96$

$37 \times 9 =$ ☐

_____

_____

$5 \cdot 8 \times 7 =$ ☐

_____

_____

_____

$0 \cdot 64 \times 9 =$ ☐

$83 \times 8 =$ ☐

_____

$6 \cdot 7 \times 5 =$ ☐

_____

_____

_____

$0 \cdot 49 \times 8 =$ ☐

$94 \times 7 =$ ☐

$47 \times 7 =$ ☐

_____

_____

_____

_____

_____

$0 \cdot 63 \times 6 =$ ☐

$99 \times 9 =$ ☐

_____

_____

$3 \cdot 9 \times 9 =$ ☐

_____

_____

_____

$0 \cdot 78 \times 6 =$ ☐

Name: _____ Date: _____

Multiplying decimals by a 1-digit number

- Multiply a decimal by a 1-digit number using the expanded written method of short multiplication
- Estimate and check the answer to a calculation.

1 Divide each number by 10.

a 56		**b** 43		**c** 256		**d** 3454	
e 872		**f** 984		**g** 1175		**h** 6543	

2 Divide each number by 100.

a 35		**b** 68		**c** 345		**d** 478	
e 3579		**f** 6328		**g** 783		**h** 4592	

3 Find the answer to these calculations using the expanded method of short multiplication. Convert the decimals to whole numbers, carry out the calculation, then convert the answer back to a decimal. Estimate the answer first.

Example

$4·63 \times 8 \rightarrow 5 \times 8 = 40$

	4	6	3
×			8
		2	4	(3 × 8)
	4	8	0	(60 × 8)
3	2	0	0	(400 × 8)
3	7	0	4
	1		

$4·63 \times 8$ is equivalent to $463 \times 8 \div 100$. This equals $3704 \div 100$, which is $37·04$

$4·63 \times 8 = 37·04$

a $3·72 \times 4 \rightarrow$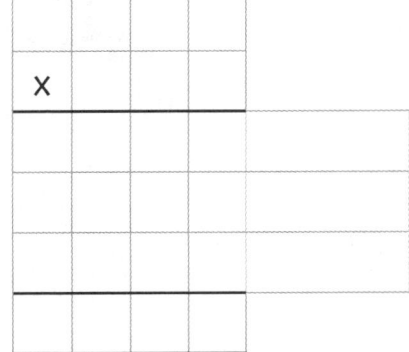

b $6·73 \times 5 \rightarrow$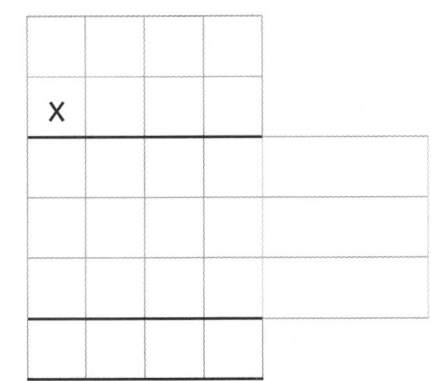

c $8·97 \times 3 \rightarrow$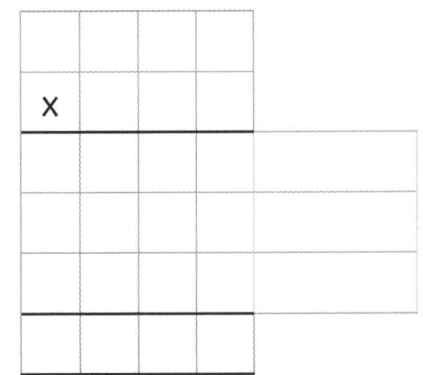

Name: _____ Date: _____

Multiplying decimals by a 1-digit number using the formal written method

- Multiply a decimal by a 1-digit number using the formal written method of short multiplication

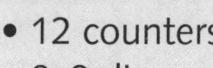

Play this game with a partner.
- Cover each item on the board with a counter.
- Take turns to:
  - remove a counter from the board
  - roll the dice
  - multiply the cost of the item by the number on the dice using the formal written method
  - say the answer to the calculation. Your partner should check the answer using a calculator.
- If you are correct, keep the counter. If you are incorrect, put the counter back on the board.
- Continue until all the counters have been removed.

  The player with the most counters at the end is the winner.

Daffodils £3.95	Lillies £18.50	Orchids £48.85	Lavender £8.79
Chrysanthemums £6.73	Roses £56.25	Sunflowers £26.60	Carnations £6.98
Flower assortment £28.56	Flower assortment in vase £76.42	Tulips £5.68	Exotic flower assortment £85.50

Name: _____ Date: _____

Domino grams and kilograms

Convert between grams and kilograms using decimals to 3 places

An activity for two players.

- Cut out the domino cards below.

- Start with the 550 g domino.

- Take turns to join a matching domino to one of the ends.

- Continue until the dominoes have made a closed rectangle, like the one on the right.

- Choose a different starting domino and make a new rectangle.

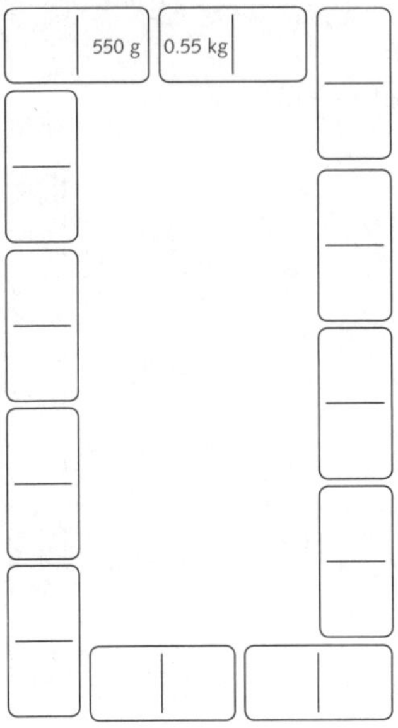

550 g	0.55 kg

170 g	0·61 kg	610 g	0·48 kg	480 g	820 g
0·82 kg	550 g	0·55 kg	750 g	0·75 kg	300 g
0·3 kg	0·25 kg	250 g	990 g	0·99 kg	0.625 kg
625 g	854 kg	0·854 g	0·026 g	26 g	0·17 kg

Name: _____ Date: _____

Mass of parcels

Convert between grams and kilograms to solve problems

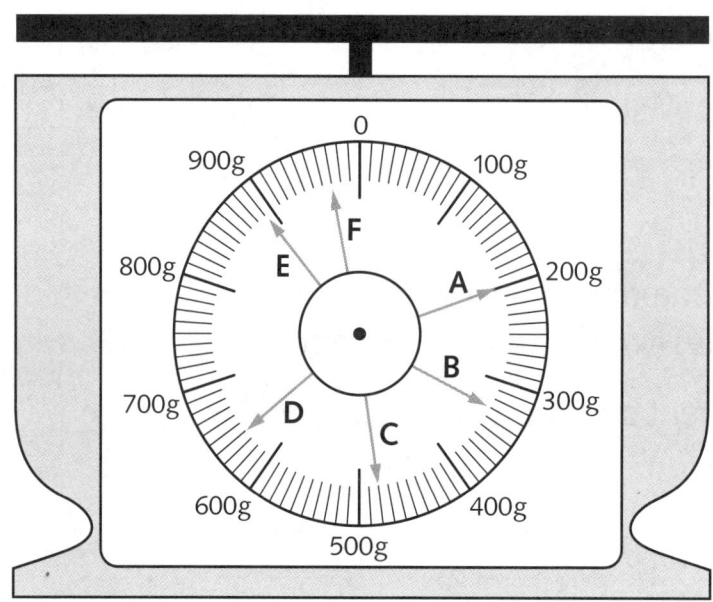

1 Complete the table. Write the mass of each parcel in grams, and then in kilograms as shown by the arrows on the scale.

Parcel	A	B	C	D	E	F
Mass (g)						
Mass (kg)						

2 Calculate the total mass of each pair of parcels in grams then convert your answer to kilograms.

   a parcels A and F [   ] g [   ] kg

   b parcels B and E [   ] g [   ] kg

   c parcels C and D [   ] g [   ] kg

3 Write the letters of the two parcels that together have the same mass as parcel F.

   parcel [   ] and parcel [   ]

Name: _____ Date: _____

ish figures

Convert between grams and kilograms to solve problems

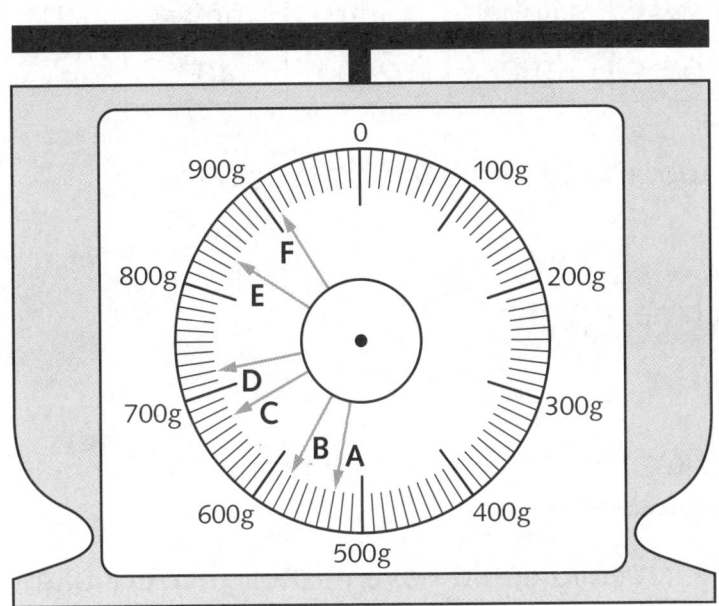

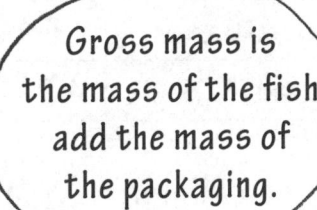

Gross mass is the mass of the fish add the mass of the packaging.

1 The arrows on the scale show the gross mass of each pack of fresh trout.
Complete the table for packs A to F of fresh trout.

Pack	Gross mass (g)	Mass of trout (g)	Mass of packaging (g)
A	530	516	
B			14
C		642	
D			28
E		798	
F			42

2 Find the total mass in kilograms of the
packaging used for all six packs. [＿＿＿] kg

3 The McDonald family enjoy trout so Mrs McDonald bought
packs C, D and E. How many kilograms of trout did she buy? [＿＿＿] kg

Name: _____ Date: _____

Delivery rounds

Convert between grams and kilograms to solve problems.

The table shows the mass of five daily newspapers.

Newspaper	Echo	Express	Globe	Star	Times
Mass (g)	240	300	150	250	400

Three children have a newspaper round and each child delivers:

- 20 newspapers

- at least two copies of each newspaper

- a different set of newspapers

- newspapers with a total mass that is greater than 4·5 kg and less than 6 kg.

Work out which newspapers each child could have in their delivery bag.

Title of newspaper	Bag 1		Bag 2		Bag 3	
	Copies	Mass (kg)	Copies	Mass (kg)	Copies	Mass (kg)
Echo						
Express						
Globe						
Star						
Times						
Totals	20		20		20	

Name: _____ Date: _____

What's the question?

Solve problems involving fractions

The mixed numbers in the circles are answers.

Write two addition calculations and two subtraction calculations for each of these mixed numbers.

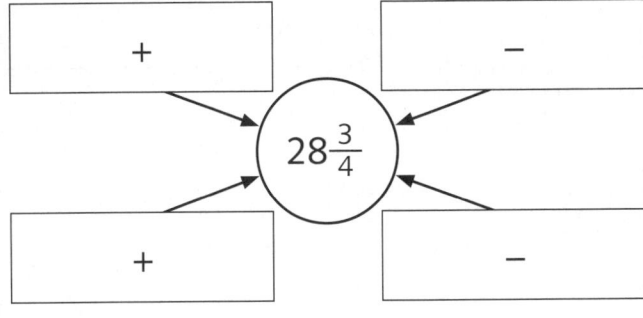

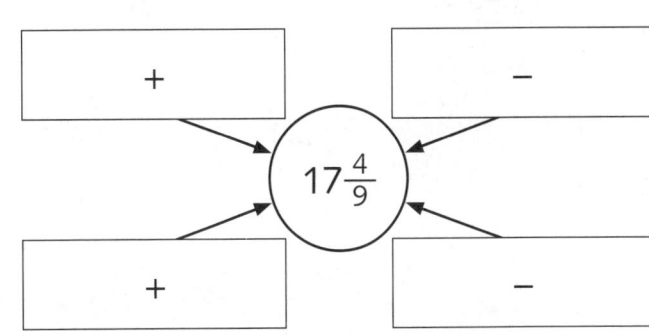

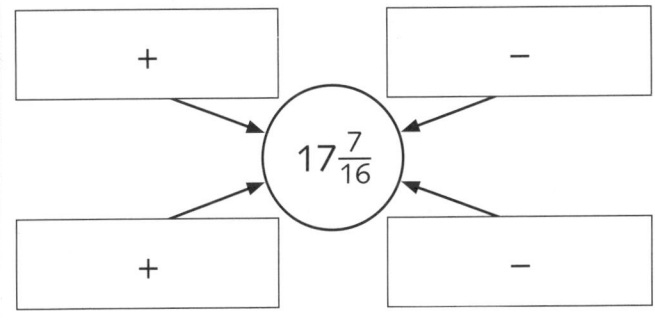

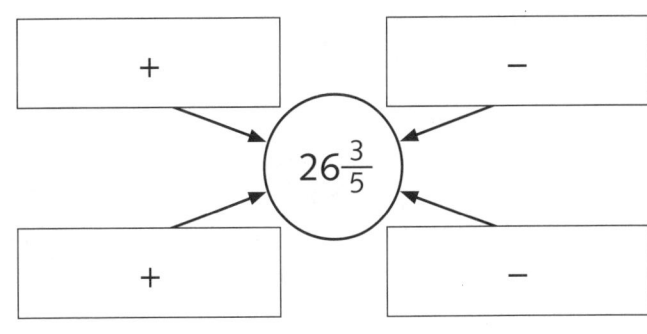

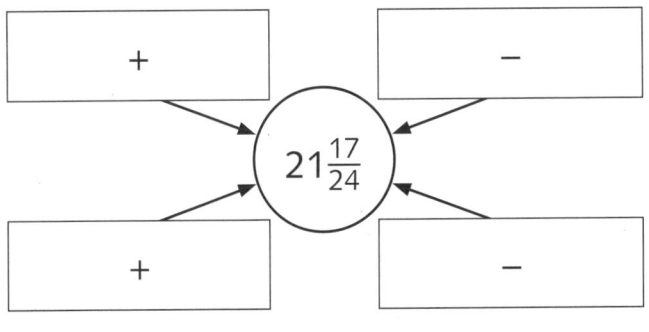

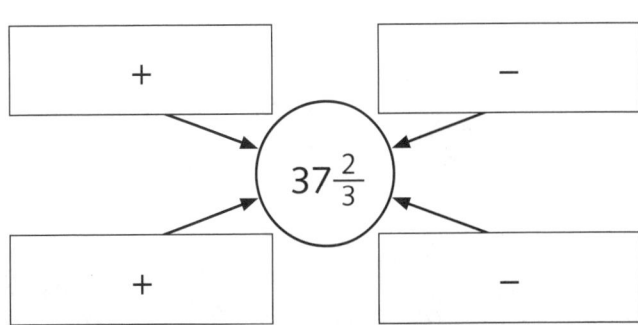

Name: _____ Date: _____

Dividing pizzas

Divide proper fractions by whole numbers

Each of these groups of children has a different fraction of pizza to share.
Work out what fraction of a whole pizza each child will eat.

Example 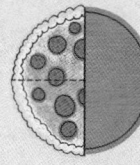   $1\frac{1}{2} \div 2 = \frac{1}{2 \times 2} = \frac{1}{4}$

a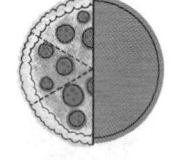

b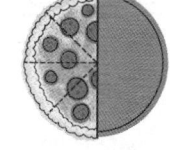

c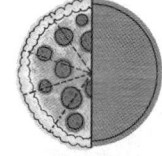

d

e

f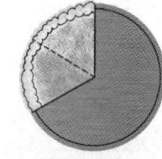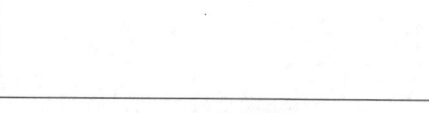

g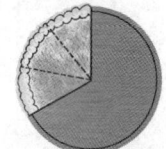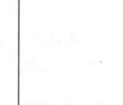

h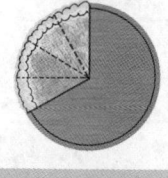

Name: _____ Date: _____

ultiplying fractions rhyme

Multiply simple pairs of proper fractions, writing
the answer in its simplest form

Work with a partner.

Think about the key steps to remember when multiplying fractions.

What mistakes do you think people make?

You could ask some of the children in your class what they find tricky.

Write a rhyme in the space below to help remember how to
multiply fractions.

You could perform it to your class.

| $\frac{1}{8}$ | $\frac{4}{12}$ | $\frac{8}{9}$ | $\frac{7}{10}$ | $\frac{6}{7}$ | $\frac{10}{16}$ | $\frac{1}{4}$ | $\frac{15}{24}$ | $\frac{5}{6}$ |

$\frac{12}{18}$ $\frac{8}{32}$

$\frac{2}{3}$ $\frac{4}{5}$

$\frac{2}{10}$ $\frac{9}{18}$

$\frac{3}{5}$ $\frac{1}{3}$

$\frac{20}{24}$ $\frac{3}{16}$

$\frac{6}{9}$ $\frac{5}{7}$

$\frac{4}{20}$ $\frac{5}{12}$

| $\frac{1}{2}$ | $\frac{12}{16}$ | $\frac{3}{4}$ | $\frac{6}{18}$ | $\frac{5}{8}$ | $\frac{20}{22}$ | $\frac{2}{6}$ | $\frac{16}{24}$ | $\frac{1}{4}$ |

Name: _____ Date: _____

Eating pizzas

Solve problems involving fractions

You will need:
• 1–6 dice
• coloured pencil

• Roll the dice and read the number as a fraction. If you roll 1, roll again.

• Shade in this amount of the first pizza. This is how much has been eaten!

• Roll the dice again. Make another fraction and shade in that amount on the same pizza.

1 What fraction of the pizza has been eaten altogether? ☐

2 What fraction is left? ☐

• Do this for every pizza.

Example
• You roll a 3 → $\frac{1}{3}$ of the pizza is eaten.

• You roll a 6 → $\frac{1}{6}$ of the pizza is eaten.

• $\frac{1}{3} + \frac{1}{6} = \frac{3}{6} = \frac{1}{2}$

• $\frac{1}{2}$ of the pizza has been eaten, and $\frac{1}{2}$ of the pizza is left

pizza eaten: ☐
pizza left: ☐

pizza eaten: ☐
pizza left: ☐

pizza eaten: ☐
pizza left: ☐

pizza eaten: ☐
pizza left: ☐

pizza eaten: ☐
pizza left: ☐

pizza eaten: ☐
pizza left: ☐

Name: _____ Date: _____

lowerbeds

Recognise and solve proportion problems

A seaside town council has agreed to plant spring flowers throughout the town. They vote to include yellow daffodils; white, purple and yellow tulips; purple irises and yellow primroses.

For every 3 daffodil bulbs, they plant 1 white tulip, 1 purple tulip, 1 yellow tulip, 2 purple irises and 4 primrose plants.

1 a What is the proportion of daffodils? ☐

   b What is the proportion of irises? ☐

   c What is the proportion of primroses? ☐

   d What is the proportion of yellow flowers? ☐

   e What is the proportion of white flowers? ☐

Show your working for questions 2 and 3 on the back of this sheet.

2 On the sea front there is a large flowerbed. The council gardeners work out that they can plant 240 plants in the bed.

   Calculate how many of each plant there will be.

3 In front of the Town Hall there is a small flower bed with 24 daffodil bulbs.

   a How many plants are in the bed altogether? ☐

   b How many tulips are there? ☐

   c How many purple tulips are there? ☐

Name: _____ Date: _____

Stripy scarves

- Use ratios to solve problems
- Solve scale factor problems

You will need:
- 2 × 1–6 dice
- ruler
- coloured pencils

Work with a partner. Begin by working separately.

- Roll the dice and note the scores.

- Work out the ratio of the two numbers in the simplest form, e.g. dice scores of 2 and 4 will give you a ratio of 1 : 2. Write the ratio in the small box.

- Choose two colours for your stripy scarf.

- In one of the boxes below, draw and colour a scarf with the correct ratios in your chosen colours.

- Try to have at least three stripes of each colour.

Now swap papers with your partner and check each other's work.

Repeat until you have drawn four different scarves. If the dice scores give a ratio that you have already drawn, roll the dice again.

Hint
Think about a suitable length to draw your scarf so that the ratios fit exactly. The scarf does not have to fill the box.

Name: _____ Date: _____

Music shop ratios

Solve ratio problems using multiplication and division

Two music stores keep their CDs arranged in the sections shown. Each store stocks their CDs in specific ratios. Use the back of this sheet for your working and complete the table for each store to show the number of CDs in each section.

a In **Store 1** the ratios are:

Pop : Hip Hop : Reggae   4 : 2 : 1   Jazz : Country : Classical   5 : 2 : 13

There is an equal number of Country, Blues and Rock CDs, and there are 80 Reggae CDs.

Pop	Hip Hop	Reggae	Jazz	Country	Classical	Blues	Rock

b In **Store 2** the ratios are different.

Pop : Jazz : Blues : Rock   6 : 4 : 2 : 3

Country : Reggae : Classical : Hip Hop   4 : 5 : 9 : 7

The number of Jazz and Hip Hop CDs are the same: 280 of each.

Pop	Hip Hop	Reggae	Jazz	Country	Classical	Blues	Rock

c Find the total numbers of Blues, Hip Hop and Classical CDs in the two shops.

Blues	Hip Hop	Classical

Now calculate the ratio of these genres in the two shops combined.

Blues : Hip Hop : Classical [ ] : [ ] : [ ]

Name: _____ Date: _____

Best value breakfast

Solve problems involving unequal sharing and grouping using knowledge of fractions and multiples

Complete the shopping list above by writing in the best value of each item, A or B from the choices in the table below.

Show your working on the back of this sheet.

Shopping list	A or B
Orange juice	
Melon	
Crunchy Cereal	
Strawberry jam	
Bread	
Butter	

	Choice A	Choice B
Orange juice	Special offer 3 × 1 litre £4.50	Giant pack 1·75 litres £3.00
Melon	Buy one 2 kg melon at £2.80, get a second one FREE	1·5 kg melon, only £1.20
Cereal	500 g box of Crunchy Cereal at £2.00	300 g box at £1.50
Strawberry jam	Tastee Strawberry Jam £1.40 for 340 g	Extra fruity Strawberry Jam £1.60 for 370 g
Bread	800 g loaf for £1.50	470 g loaf for 80p
Butter	125 g butter for £1.10	2 packs of 250 g butter for £3.20

Sometimes supermarkets display labels showing the cost of 100 g for different size packets to help you compare values. Look out for them next time you are in the supermarket.

Name: _____ Date: _____

ata in pie charts

Interpret and draw pie charts and use them to solve problems

Each sector in these pie charts represents 10%.

1 The pie chart shows the percentage of pets kept by children in a Year 6 class.

What percentage of pets were:

a cats [ ] %   **b** dogs [ ] %

c birds [ ] %   **d** rabbits [ ] %

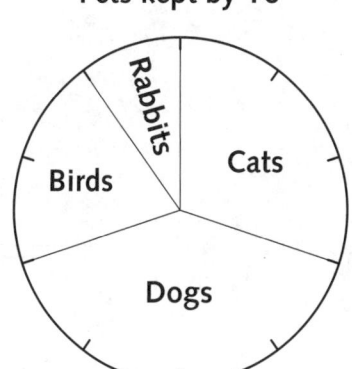
Pets kept by Y6
(Rabbits, Birds, Cats, Dogs)

2 The pie chart shows the percentage of favourite drinks of children in a Year 6 class.

What percentage of their choices were:

a tea [ ] %   **b** milk [ ] %

c coffee [ ] %   **d** cola [ ] %

Favourite drinks
(Tea, Cola, Coffee, Milk)

3 The table shows the percentage of each colour of cars in a supermarket car park.

a Use the percentages in the table to complete the pie chart.

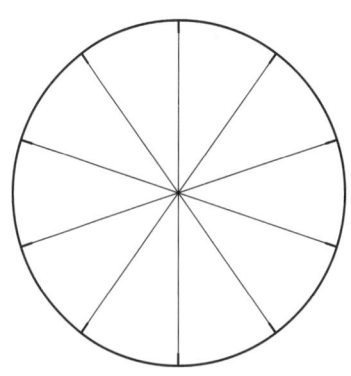
Colours of cars

Colour of car	red	blue	white	black
Percentage (%)	30	10	40	20

b What percentage of cars in the car park were not white? [ ] %

Name: _____ Date: _____

Driving lessons pie chart

Interpret and draw pie charts and use them to solve problems

The pie chart shows the driving lessons given by an instructor from April to September. Each sector in the pie chart represents 5%.

Driving lessons given

1 What percentage of driving lessons were given in:

   a April [ ] %

   b August [ ] %

   c June [ ] %

2 If the instructor gave 90 driving lessons in June, how many lessons did he give in:

   a August? [ ]

   b May? [ ]

   c September? [ ]

3 How many more driving lessons did he give in July than in June? [ ]

4 How many lessons altogether did the instructor give for the 6 months from April to September? [ ]

5 In which month did the instructor take time out for a holiday? _____

   Give a reason for your answer.

_____

_____

Name: _____ Date: _____

ind the mean scores

Calculate the mean as an average of a set of data

1 Cut out the 20 cards below.
Shuffle the cards and place them face down on the table, making five rows of four cards.

2 Turn over the cards in the first row.
Find the mean score of your cards by:

- finding the total of the four cards
- dividing the total by four.

Example

2 + 4 + 7 + 9 = 22

22 ÷ 4 = 5·5

Record your numbers and answers in the grid below.

3 Repeat Step 2 for each of the remaining four rows of cards.

Row	Cards				Total	Mean
Example	2	4	7	9	22	5.5
1						
2						
3						
4						
5						

1	2	3	4	3
6	4	8	5	10
6	12	7	14	8
16	9	18	10	20

Name: _____ Date: _____

2-digit mean scores

Calculate the mean as an average of a set of data

You will need:
• scissors

1 Cut out the 24 cards below.
Shuffle the cards and place them face down on the table, making six rows of four cards.

2 Turn over the cards in the first row. Find the mean score of your cards by:

• finding the total of the four cards
• dividing the total by four.

Record your numbers and answers in the grid below.

3 Repeat Step 2 for each of the remaining five rows of cards.

Example

12 + 54 + 15 + 81 = 162

162 ÷ 4 = 40·5

Row	Cards				Total	Mean
Example	12	54	15	81	162	40·5
1						
2						
3						
4						
5						
6						

40	15	20	36	10	60
42	50	12	30	18	54
16	24	45	48	63	56
70	14	28	35	72	81

Name: _____ Date: _____

ivision HTO ÷ TO using the expanded written method

- Use the expanded written method of long division to calculate HTO ÷ TO
- Estimate and check the answer to a calculation

For each division calculation write your estimate, then use the expanded written method to work out the answer.

Example

644 ÷ 14 → 600 ÷ 10 = 60

	H	T	O	
		4	6	
1 4	6	4	4	
−	5	6	0	(40 × 14)
		8	4	
−		8	4	(6 × 14)
			0	

a 560 ÷ 16 →

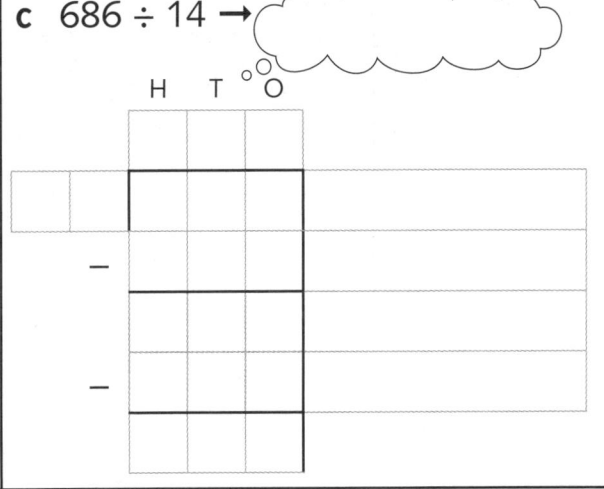

b 495 ÷ 15 →

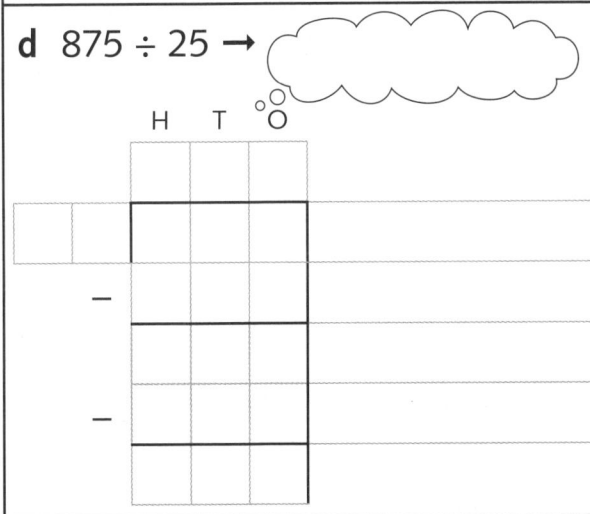

c 686 ÷ 14 →

d 875 ÷ 25 →

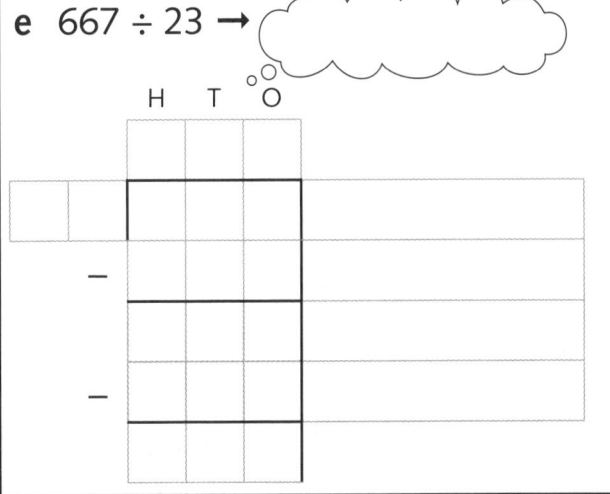

e 667 ÷ 23 →

Name: _____ Date: _____

Division ThHTO ÷ TO using the expanded written method

- Use the expanded written method of long division to calculate ThHTO ÷ TO
- Estimate and check the answer to a calculation

For each division calculation write your estimate, then use the expanded written method to work out the answer.

Example

$5832 \div 18 \rightarrow$ ($6000 \div 20 = 300$)

		Th	H	T	O	
			3	2	4	
1	8	5	8	3	2	
	−	5	4	0	0	(300 × 18)
			³4	¹³3	2	
	−		3	6	0	(20 × 18)
				7	2	
	−			7	2	(4 × 18)
					0	

a $5310 \div 15 \rightarrow$

b $6118 \div 14 \rightarrow$

c $7898 \div 22 \rightarrow$

d $8432 \div 16 \rightarrow$

Name: _____ Date: _____

ivision ThHTO ÷ TO using the expanded written method

- Use the expanded written method of long division to calculate ThHTO ÷ TO
- Estimate and check the answer to a calculation

For each division calculation write your estimate, then use the expanded written method to work out the answer. Check your answer using the multiplication inverse.

Example

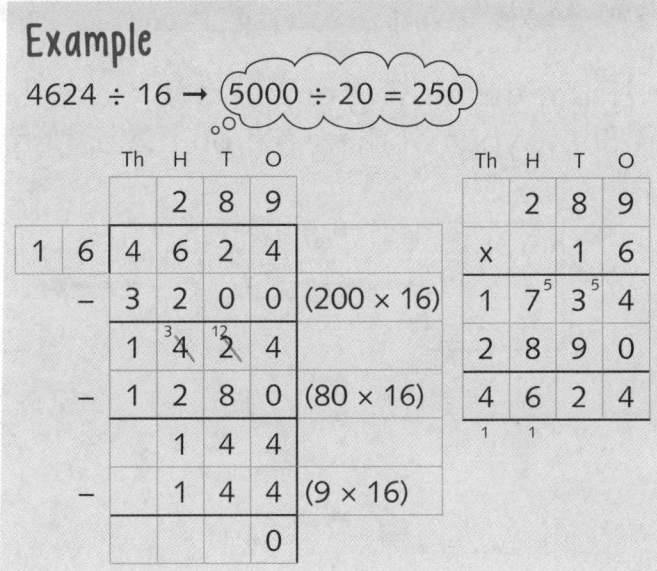

$4624 ÷ 16 →$ (5000 ÷ 20 = 250)

Th	H	T	O	
	2	8	9	
1 6	4	6	2	4
− 3	2	0	0	(200 × 16)
1	³4	¹²2	4	
− 1	2	8	0	(80 × 16)
	1	4	4	
−	1	4	4	(9 × 16)
			0	

Th	H	T	O
	2	8	9
×		1	6
1	7⁵	3⁵	4
2	8	9	0
4	6	2	4
	₁	₁	

a 6821 ÷ 19 →

Th H T O

b 7784 ÷ 28 →

Th H T O

c 9672 ÷ 39 →

Th H T O

d 9612 ÷ 27 →

Th H T O

Name: _____ Date: _____

Number pathways

- Use the formal written methods of multiplication and long division calculate
  ThHTO ÷ TO
- Use the inverse relationship between multiplication and division

Fill in the missing numbers to make the number pathways complete.
Show your working out on the back of this sheet.

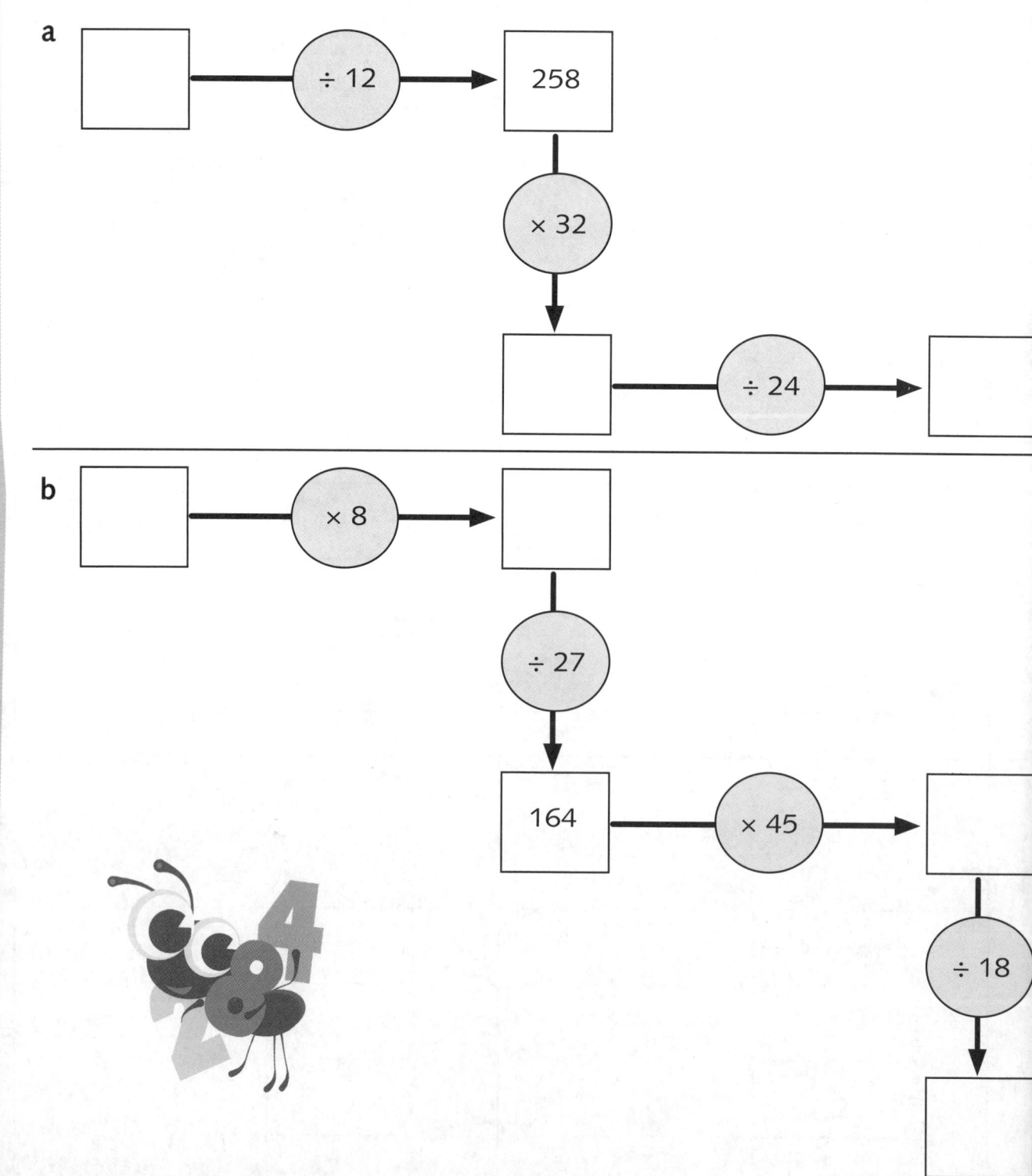

Name: _____ Date: _____

Dividing decimals using mental methods

Use mental methods to divide a decimal by a 1-digit number

Look at the start number. Follow the instructions at the top of each box to find each number until you reach the finish.

Start								Finish
6	× 10	÷ 100	× 100	× 10	÷ 10	÷ 100	× 100	÷ 10	
7	× 100	÷ 10	÷ 100	× 10	÷ 100	× 10	÷ 10	× 100	
3	× 8	÷ 10	÷ 6	× 12	÷ 8	× 7	÷ 10	× 100	
9	× 12	÷ 10	÷ 2	÷ 9	× 6	× 10	× 3	÷ 12	

Name: _____ Date: _____

Dividing decimals using the expanded written method of long division

- Use the expanded written method of long division to divide a decimal by a 2-digit number
- Estimate and check the answer to a calculation

For each division calculation your estimate, then use the expanded written method to work out the answer. Choose your preferred method.

Example

58·32 ÷ 18 is equivalent to 5832 ÷ 18 ÷ 100

5832 ÷ 18 → 6000 ÷ 20 = 300

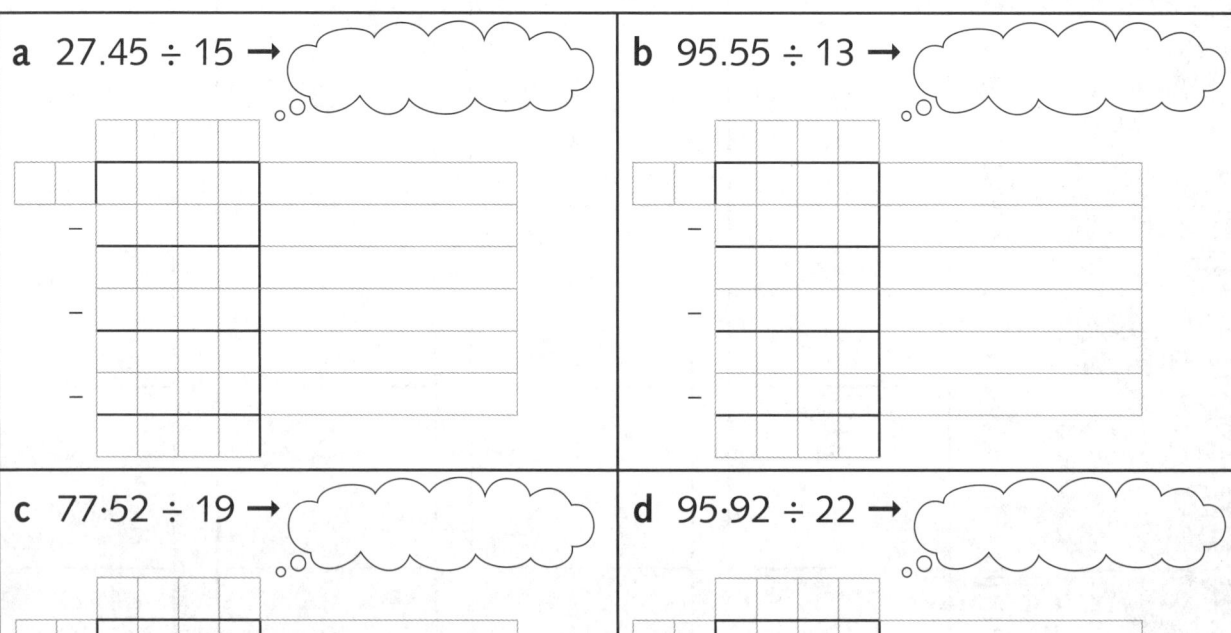

		3	2	4	
1	8	5	8	3	2
	−	5	4	0	0	(300 × 18)
			³4	⁴3	2
	−		3	6	0	(20 × 18)
				7	2
	−			7	2	(4 × 18)
					0

or

		3 ·	2	4	
1	8	5	8 ·	3	2
	−	5	4 ·	0	0	(3 × 18)
			³4 ·	⁴3	2
	−		3 ·	6	0	(0·2 × 18)
			0 ·	7	2
	−		0 ·	7	2	(0·04 × 18)
			0 ·	0	0

324 ÷ 100 = 3·24

a 27.45 ÷ 15 →

b 95.55 ÷ 13 →

c 77·52 ÷ 19 →

d 95·92 ÷ 22 →

Name: _____ Date: _____

andle problems

- Solve word problem involving the four operations
- Estimate and check the answer to a calculation

pencil taper candles (pack of 14) **£8.54**	liquid wax tea lights (pack of 15) **£54.90**	dinner table candles (pack of 25) **£38.50**	scented candles (pack of 24) **£64.32**	floating candles (pack of 12) **£14.28**

Answer to these word problems. Remember to use estimation to check your answers.

a How much does one liquid wax tea light cost?	**b** You buy a pack of dinner table candles and use three candles each mealtime. What is the cost of candles per mealtime?
c What is the cost of one taper candle?	**d** If you buy 84 taper candles in total and 75 tea lights in total, how much do you spend?
e Scented candles are on sale at a discount of 25% off the normal price. If you buy one pack, how much do you save? What is the new price?	**f** You buy one pack of each type of candle. **a** How much do you spend? **b** How many candles do you have altogether?
g You buy three packs from the candle shop. You pay with two £50 notes and receive £8.72 change. Which packs did you buy?	**h** You have a £200 voucher buy any candles you like in any quantities. What would you buy? Try to get as close to £200 as possible as you will not receive any change!

Name: _____ Date: _____

Car troubles

- Solve word problems involving the four operations
- Estimate and check the answer to a calculation

Answer these problems. Remember to use estimation to check your answers. Show your working out on the back of this sheet.

£8796

1 Mrs Ryan bought her car for £8796. She paid for it with 6 monthly payments. She had to pay an additional interest cost of one tenth of each monthly payment. How much did she pay per month?

£ _____

£7875

2 Sarah bought her car at a cost of £7875. She paid for it over 9 months at an additional cost of 20% of each monthly payment.
a How much did she pay per month?
b What was the total cost of the car?

£ _____

£6486

3 Mr Turner bought his car for £6486. He paid for it over 8 months. He had to pay an additional interest cost of one quarter of each monthly payment.
a How much did he pay per month to the nearest penny?
b What did the car cost in total?

£ _____

£ _____

£9368

4 Rajeev bought his car for £9368. He paid for it up front and received a discount worth 25% of the price.
a What was the discount?
b How much did he pay for his car?

£ _____

Name: _____ Date: _____

ame perimeter

Know that shapes with the same perimeters can have different areas and vice versa

These shapes have the same perimeter but they have different areas.

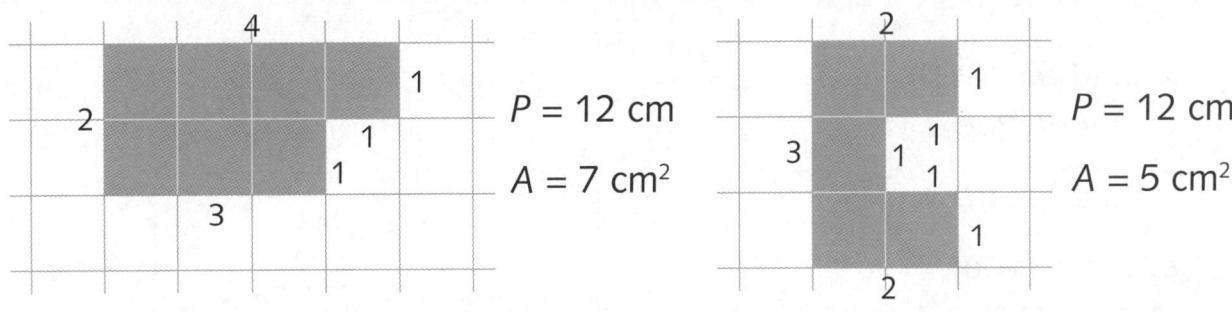

$P = 12$ cm

$A = 7$ cm²

$P = 12$ cm

$A = 5$ cm²

1 Find the perimeter and area of these shapes. Each grid square is 1 cm across.

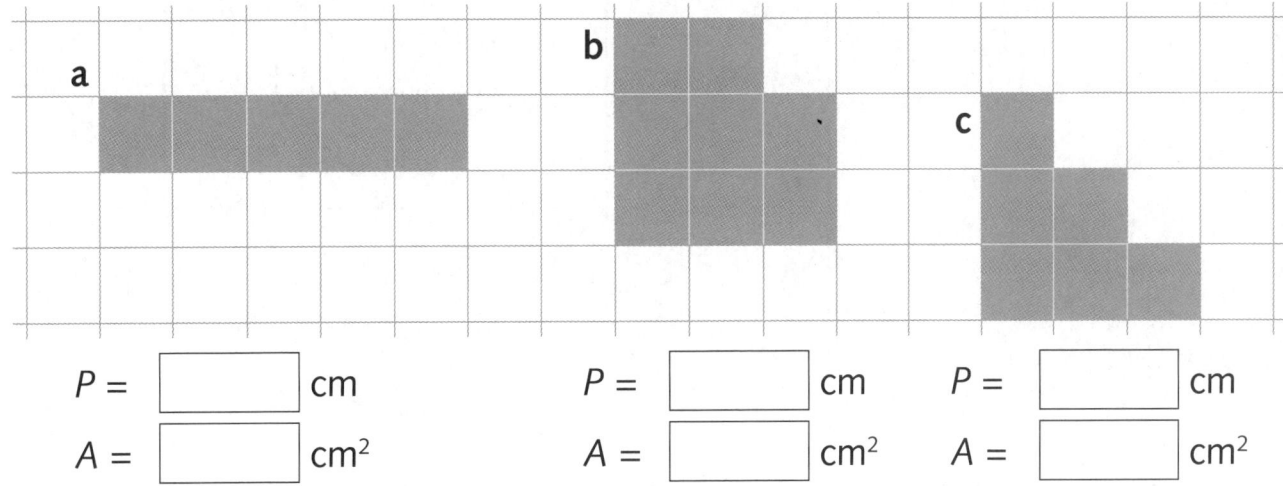

a

b

c

$P = $ [ ] cm $\quad\quad$ $P = $ [ ] cm $\quad\quad$ $P = $ [ ] cm

$A = $ [ ] cm² $\quad\quad$ $A = $ [ ] cm² $\quad\quad$ $A = $ [ ] cm²

2 Draw three more shapes that have a perimeter of 12 cm.

Find the area of each shape. Each grid square is 1 cm across.

Name: _____ Date: _____

Investigating the area of squares

Know when to use the formula for the area of shapes

1 For each square A to F:

   a find the length of one side

   b find the perimeter

   c record your answer in the table below.

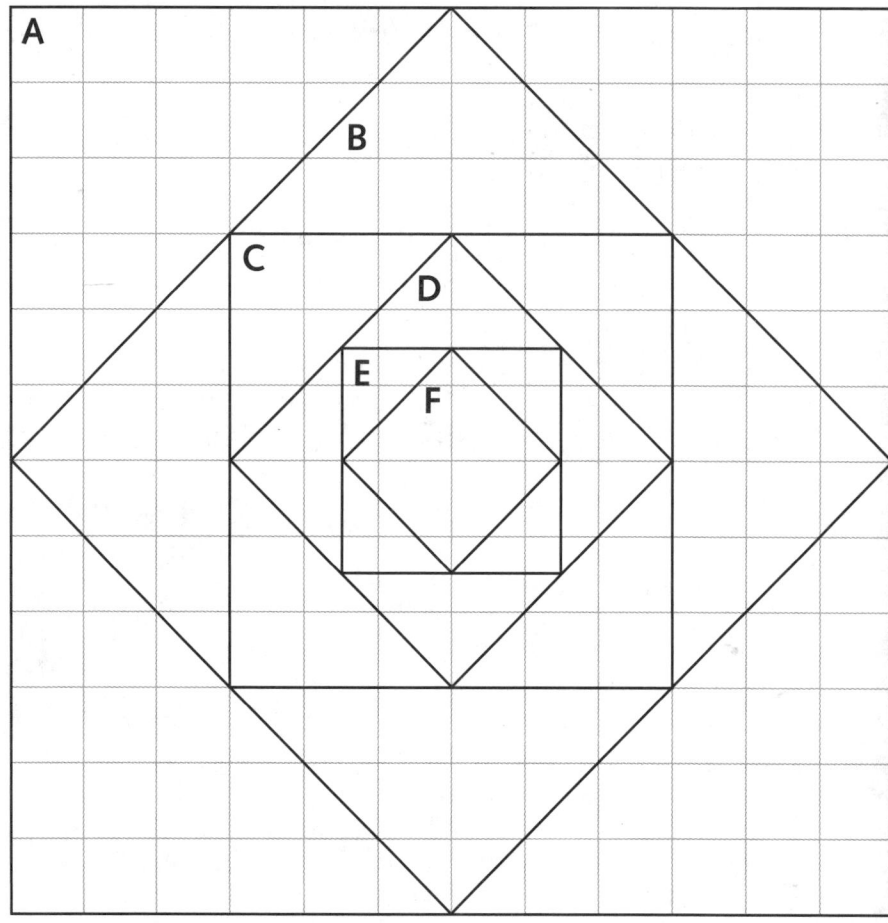

Square	A	B	C	D	E	F
Length of side (cm)	12	8·5				
Perimeter (cm)	48					
Area (cm²)	144					

2 Find the area of squares A, C and E and write them in the table.

3 Write what you notice about your results for squares A, C and E.

_____

4 Predict the perimeter and area for square G.   Perimeter = ☐ cm

                                                        Area = ☐ cm²

Name: _____ Date: _____

ot grid areas

Calculate the area of a triangle using the rule $A = \frac{1}{2}bh$

1 For each dot grid:
- draw lines to make a rectangle

You will need:
- ruler

- find and record the area of the triangle in square centimetres.

The pins are 1 cm apart.

a
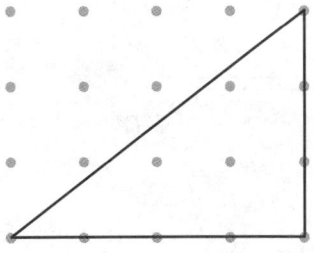

Area = [   ] cm²

b
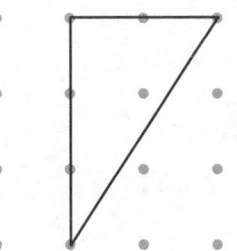

Area = [   ] cm²

c
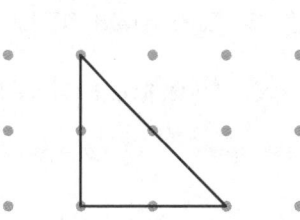

Area = [   ] cm²

d
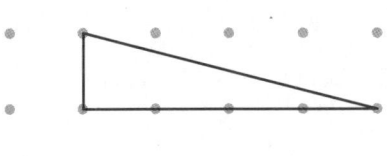

Area = [   ] cm²

e
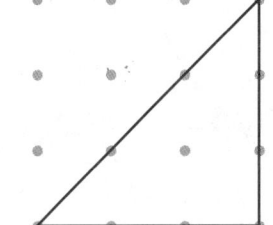

Area = [   ] cm²

f
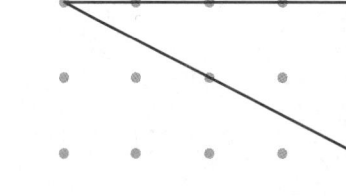

Area = [   ] cm²

g
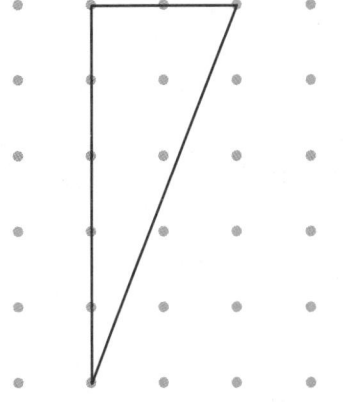

Area = [   ] cm²

h
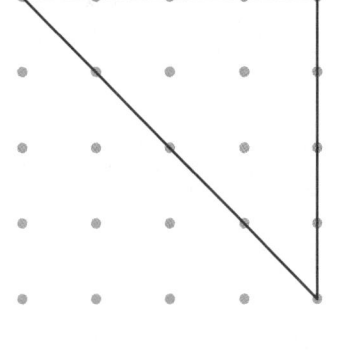

Area = [   ] cm²

i
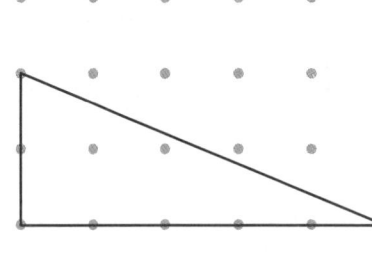

Area = [   ] cm²

Name: _____ Date: _____

Puzzling pieces

Calculate the area of a triangle using the rule $A = \frac{1}{2}bh$

You will need:
• scissors

1 Shape A has sides of 4 cm and an area of 16 cm². Cut out the shapes, then use:

    a the area of A to find the area of B   B = ☐ cm²

    b the area of B to find the area of D   D = ☐ cm²

    c the area of D to find the area of E   E = ☐ cm²

    d the area of B to find the area of C.   C = ☐ cm²

2 a Make a triangle with shapes A, B and E.   Area of triangle = ☐ cm²

    b Make a square with shapes B, C, D and E. Area of square = ☐ cm²

    c Use all five shapes to make a square.   Area of square = ☐ cm²

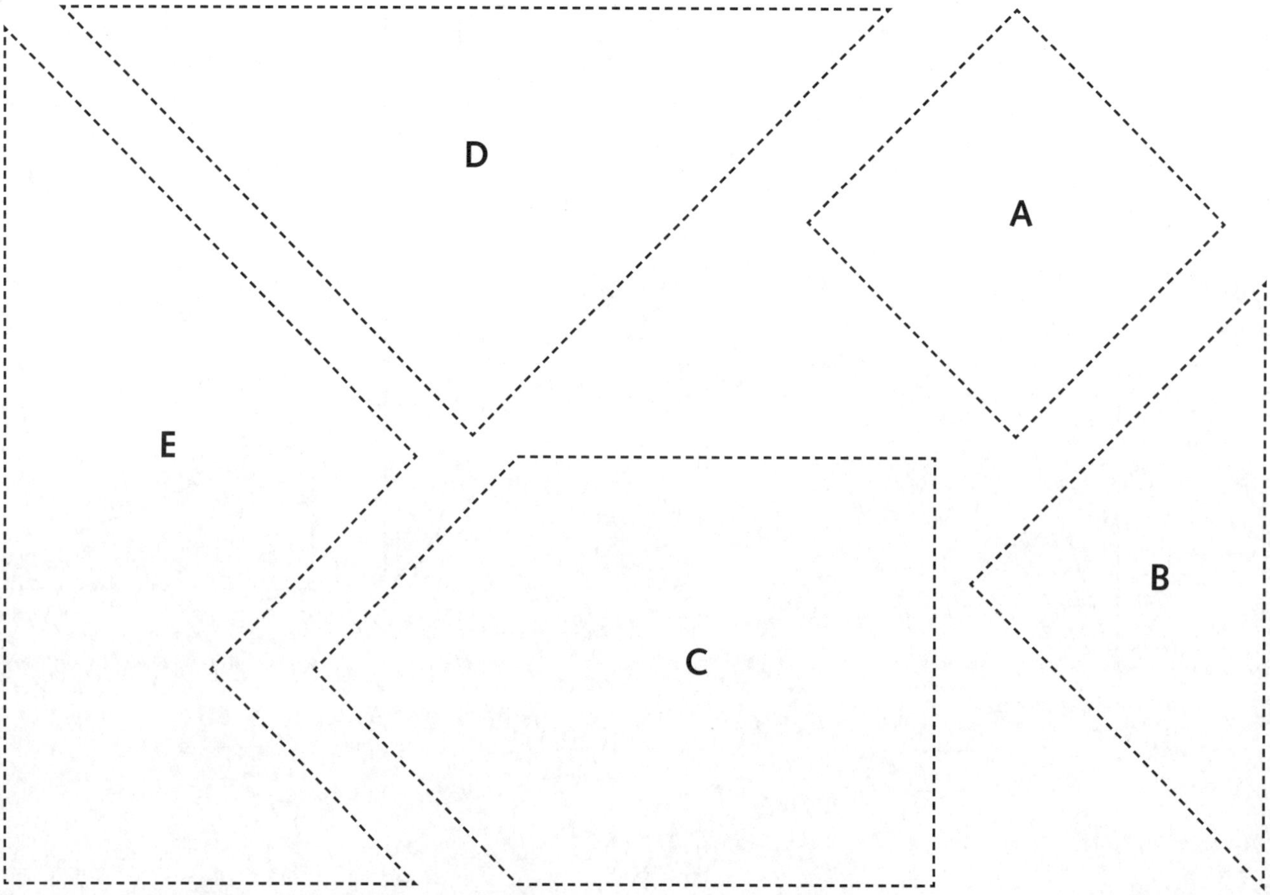

D

A

E

B

C

Name: _____ Date: _____

ace to 500 000

Perform mental calculations including large numbers

Either race on your own or against a partner.

- 100 000 is your start number.
- Spin the spinner and roll the dice.
- Put the results together to make a number.
- Add the number on to your start number.
  Write your number in the table below.
- Keep going until your number is higher than 500 000.

If you are playing with a partner, the winner is
the first player whose number is higher than 500 000.

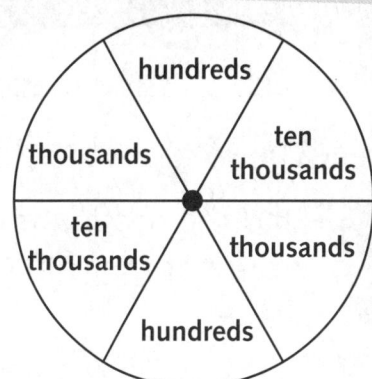

Game 1 or Player 1

Hundred thousand	Ten thousand	Thousand	Hundreds	Tens	Ones
1	0	0	0	0	0

I rolled 2 and spun 'ten thousands' so my number is 20 000.

Game 2 or Player 2

- Play again on the back of this sheet.

- Start from 500 000 and use subtraction.

Hundred thousand	Ten thousand	Thousand	Hundreds	Tens	Ones
1	0	0	0	0	0

Name: _____ Date: _____

Shape values

- Add and subtract whole numbers mentally and using the formal written methods of columnar addition and subtraction
- Estimate and check the answer to a calculation

Each of these shapes has a numerical value.

The total for the shapes is written at the end of each row and column.

Find the missing total and work out the value of each shape.

When you have finished, put the value of each shape back into the grid and check the totals for each row and column are correct.

■	●	●	■	= 77 000
▲	●	▲	●	= 91 000
★	■	★	★	= 48 500
★	●	★	★	= 47 000
= ☐	= 75 500	= 64 500	= 57 500	

■ = ☐
● = ☐
▲ = ☐
★ = ☐

Think about the value for each shape.

Compare the totals of the rows and columns to help you.

When you have completed the grid, add the four 5-digit numbers along the bottom of the grid. Then add the four 5-digit numbers down the right-hand side of the grid. What do you notice?'

Name: _____ Date: _____

BODMAS rules!

Use knowledge of the order of operations to carry out calculations involving the four operations

Use the BODMAS rule to work out the answers to these calculations.

a 335 + 6 × 20 =

b 57 − 9 × 3 =

c 72 + 36 ÷ 4 =

d 78 − 36 ÷ 6 =

e 99 ÷ 11 − 2 =

f 8 × 4 + 16 =

g 75 − (38 + 10) =

h 640 ÷ (5 + 5) =

i 8 × (24 − 3) =

j 51 × (3 + 2) =

k (50 − 36) × 2 =

l (145 − 127) ÷ 9 =

BODMAS

B   **B**rackets

O   **O**rders (e.g. 4^2)

DM Division and **M**ultiplication

AS Addition and **S**ubtraction

Working out

Name: _____ Date: _____

Franco's Chairs

Solve problems involving addition, subtraction, multiplication and division

Franco decides that his cafes need some new chairs.

There are two designs he really likes.

Franco spends exactly £5000 on a mixture of the two designs of chairs.

How many of each design does he buy?

Show your working out in the box below.

Fun style
£180

Country style £260

Hint
There are two possible answers. Have you found them both?

Working out

Name: _____ Date: _____

Collecting terms and using brackets

- Use simple formulae
- Generate and describe linear number sequences

You will need:
- scissors
- 1–6 dice
- pencil and paper

Two games to play with a partner for five minutes each.

Game 1
- Cut out and shuffle the cards. Put them in piles of each size.
- Choose a large card and two small cards and write the expression on the sheet of paper.
- Simplify it. Roll the dice twice. The first roll is the value for a and the second roll is the value for b.
- Solve the expression using these values.

Game 2
- Cut out and shuffle the cards. Put them in separate piles of x, y and numbers.
- Choose one card from each pile.
- Put the number card outside the bracket and the x and y cards inside the brackets.
- Multiply out the brackets.

$$\boxed{} \left(\boxed{} + \boxed{} \right)$$

Game 1 cards

$- 2a$	$- a$	$- 3a$
$- b$	$- 3b$	$- 4b$

$6a$	$8a$
$9b$	$10b$

Game 2 cards

$3x$	x	$4x$	$6x$	$10x$
$2y$	$5y$	y	$3y$	$8y$
1	3	5	7	9

Name: _____ Date: _____

Serpent algebra

- Use simple formulae
- Generate and describe linear number sequences

You will need:
- 1 cm squared paper
- ruler

Squarey serpents have bodies and heads made from squares. There are three types of serpents, each with different sized heads. The smallest body size is two squares.

One-headed serpents have a head of one square	Two-headed serpents have a head of two squares joined corner to corner	Three-headed serpents have a head of three squares joined corner to corner
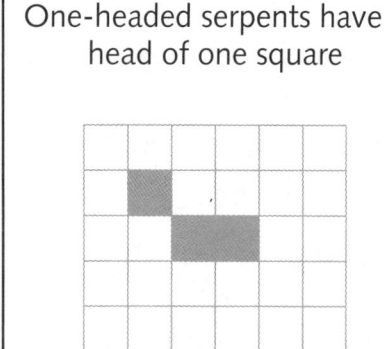	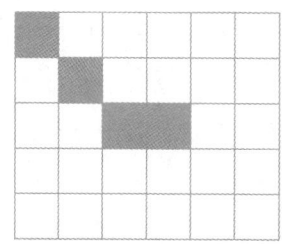	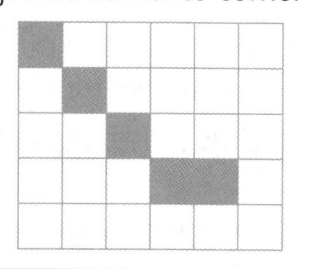

a Use squared paper to draw one-headed serpents with bodies of 2, 3, 4 and 5 squares.

b Complete the table for one-headed serpents and work out an expression for a serpent with body size *b*.

c Use this expression to write equations for *s*, the number of squares and *p*, the perimeter.

d Predict the perimeter of a one-headed serpent with body size 9. Draw it to check your prediction.

e Complete the table for two-headed serpents.

One-headed serpents

Body size (*b*)	2	3	4	5	*b*
Number of squares (*s*)					
Perimeter (*p*)					

Two-headed serpents

Body size (*b*)	2	3	4	5	*b*
Number of squares (*s*)					
Perimeter (*p*)					

Three-headed serpents

Body size (*b*)	2	3	4	5	*b*
Number of squares (*s*)					
Perimeter (*p*)					

f Complete the table for three-headed serpents.

g Using these values, work out the general rule for the perimeter, *p*, of an *x*-headed serpent of body size *b*.

Name: _____ Date: _____

Algebra puzzle squares

- Find pairs of numbers that satisfy an equation with two unknowns
- Use simple formulae

Each of these shapes has a numerical value. The total for the shapes is written at the end of each row and column. Find the missing totals and work out the value of each shape.

a

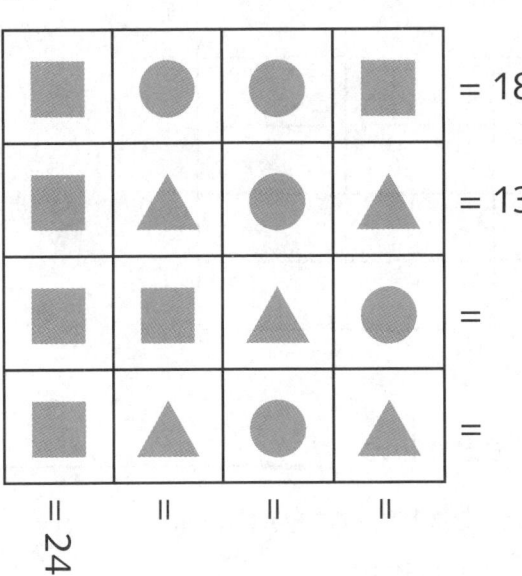

b

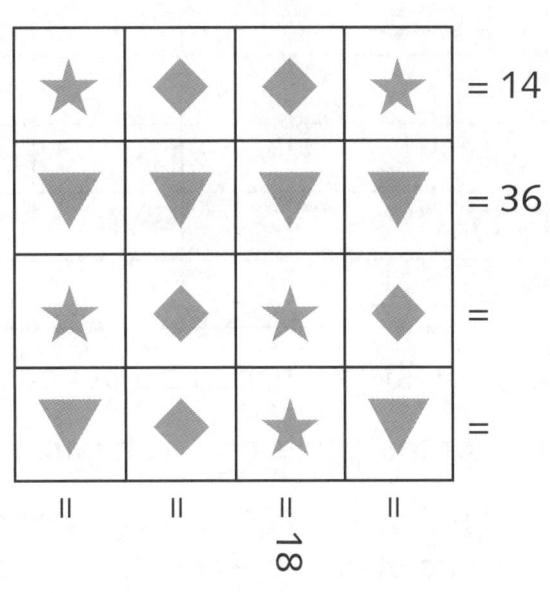

c

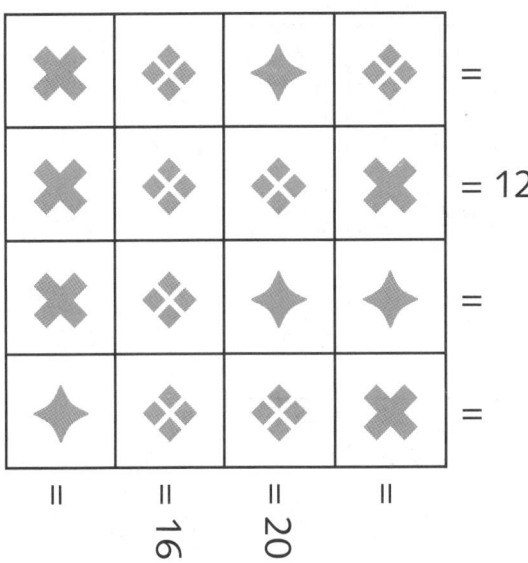

d

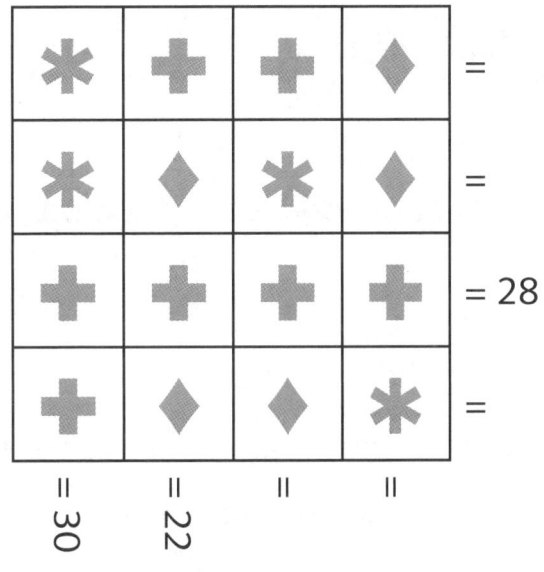

Name: _____ Date: _____

Gradients

- Find pairs of numbers that satisfy an equation with two unknowns
- Use simple formulae

You will need:
- graph paper
- ruler

1 a Complete the table and find values for y when $x = 1, 2, 3$ and 4.

Line equation		$x = 1$	$x = 2$	$x = 3$	$x = 4$
$y = x + 2$	$y =$				
$y = 2x + 2$	$y =$				
$y = 3x + 2$	$y =$				
$y = 4x + 2$	$y =$				
$y = 5x + 2$	$y =$				

b Describe the patterns that you notice.

c Plot the results on graph paper. Label each line. _____

d On the back of this sheet, describe what happens to the line as the value of m in the equation $y = mx + 2$ increases.

e Predict the slope of the line if the value of x is less than 1.

_____

2 Complete this table and plot the line.

Line equation		$x = 0$	$x = 2$	$x = 4$	$x = 6$
$y = \frac{1}{2}x + 2$	$y =$				

What has happened to the slope of the line? _____
Well done if your prediction was correct!

f Plot the line $y = x + 6$. Label the line. Find three values for y. What do you notice about the line? _____

g Predict a line equation that is parallel to $y = 2x + 2$.

h Calculate points on the line you predicted in **g** and plot them to see if you are correct. Label your line.

Name: _____ Date: _____

exagon patterns

Use compasses to construct a regular hexagon and
patterns based on the hexagon

You will need:
- compasses
- ruler
- sharp pencil
- coloured pencils

Set your compasses to a radius of 2 cm.
Use the space below to draw your pattern.

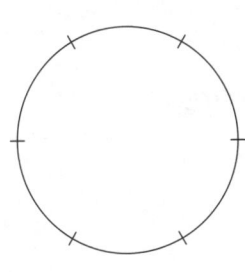

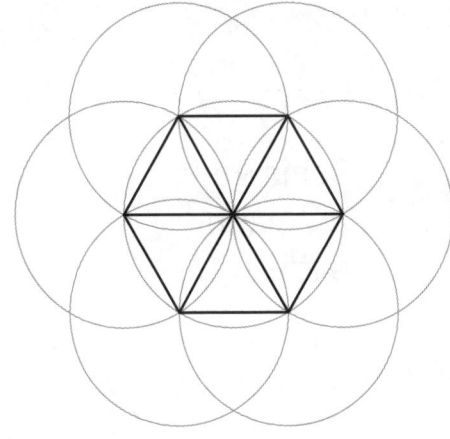

Step 1 Draw a circle
and mark off
six points on the
circumference.

Step 2 Using each point as a
centre, construct six
more circles.

Step 3 Rule the lines as shown
above to complete the
pattern. Then colour
your pattern.

Working out

Name: _____ Date: _____

Circle designs

Use compasses to construct a regular hexagon
and patterns based on the hexagon

You will need:
- compasses
- ruler
- coloured pencils
- blank paper
- eraser

Use compasses and a ruler to construct these
shapes on blank paper.

1 Begin with   Erase some lines …   and some more.
the basic
pattern …

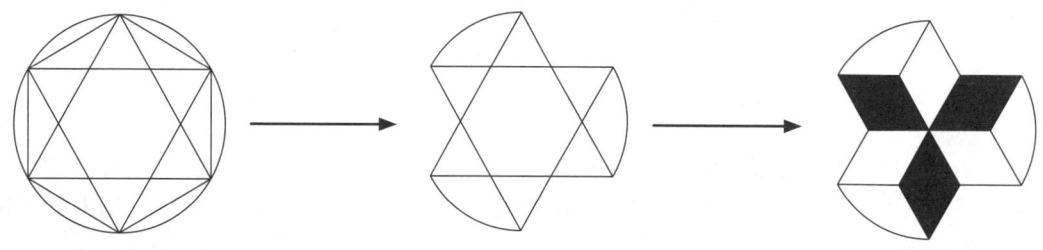

2 Again, begin   Erase some lines …   Draw some lines …
with the basic   and part of the circle.   Then add colour.
pattern …

3 Work out how these designs have been made. Choose three designs and
construct them on blank paper. Use a radius of 3 cm. Colour your patterns.

Name: _____ Date: _____

atterns in a circle

Construct patterns that are based on the radius of a circle

You will need:
• coloured
  pencils

For each circle, use your
coloured pencils to make
a different pattern.

a

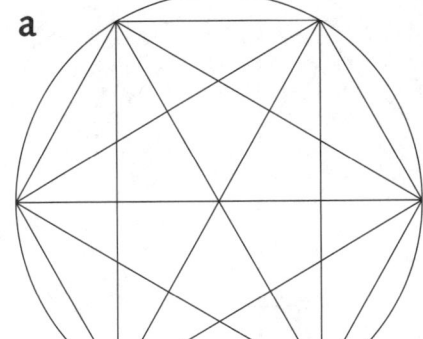

b

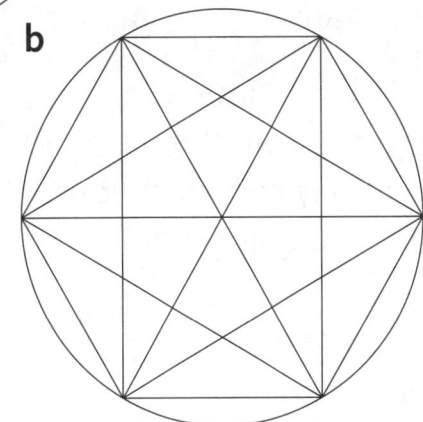

c

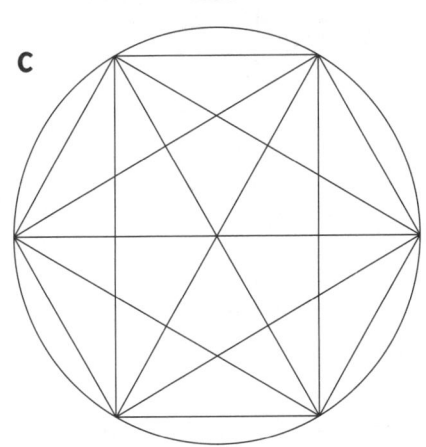

d

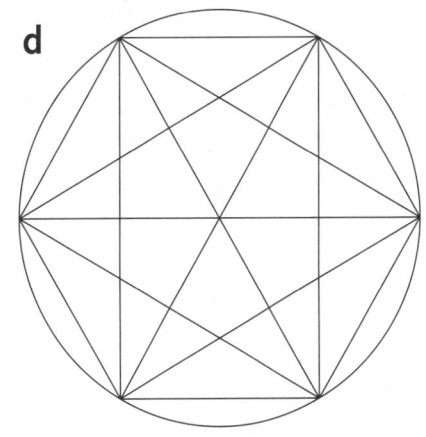

e

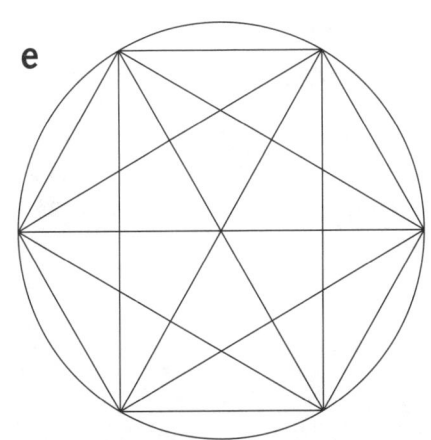

f

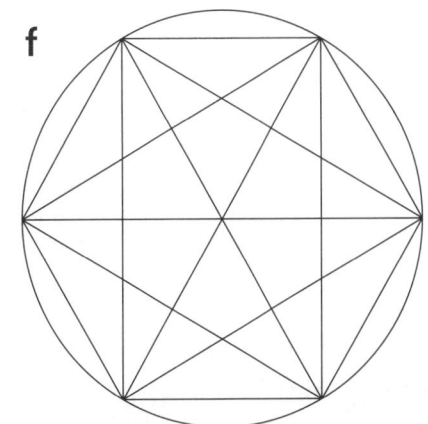

Name: _____ Date: _____

Egg tangrams

Use compasses to construct patterns that are based on the radius of a circle

1 This diagram shows how to make an egg tangram.

- The circle has a radius of 5 cm.

- The diameters are at right angles.

- All acute angles equal 45°.

- Each arc from A to B and from C to D has a radius of 10 cm.

Work out how to draw the arc from B to D. Now carefully construct your own egg tangram.

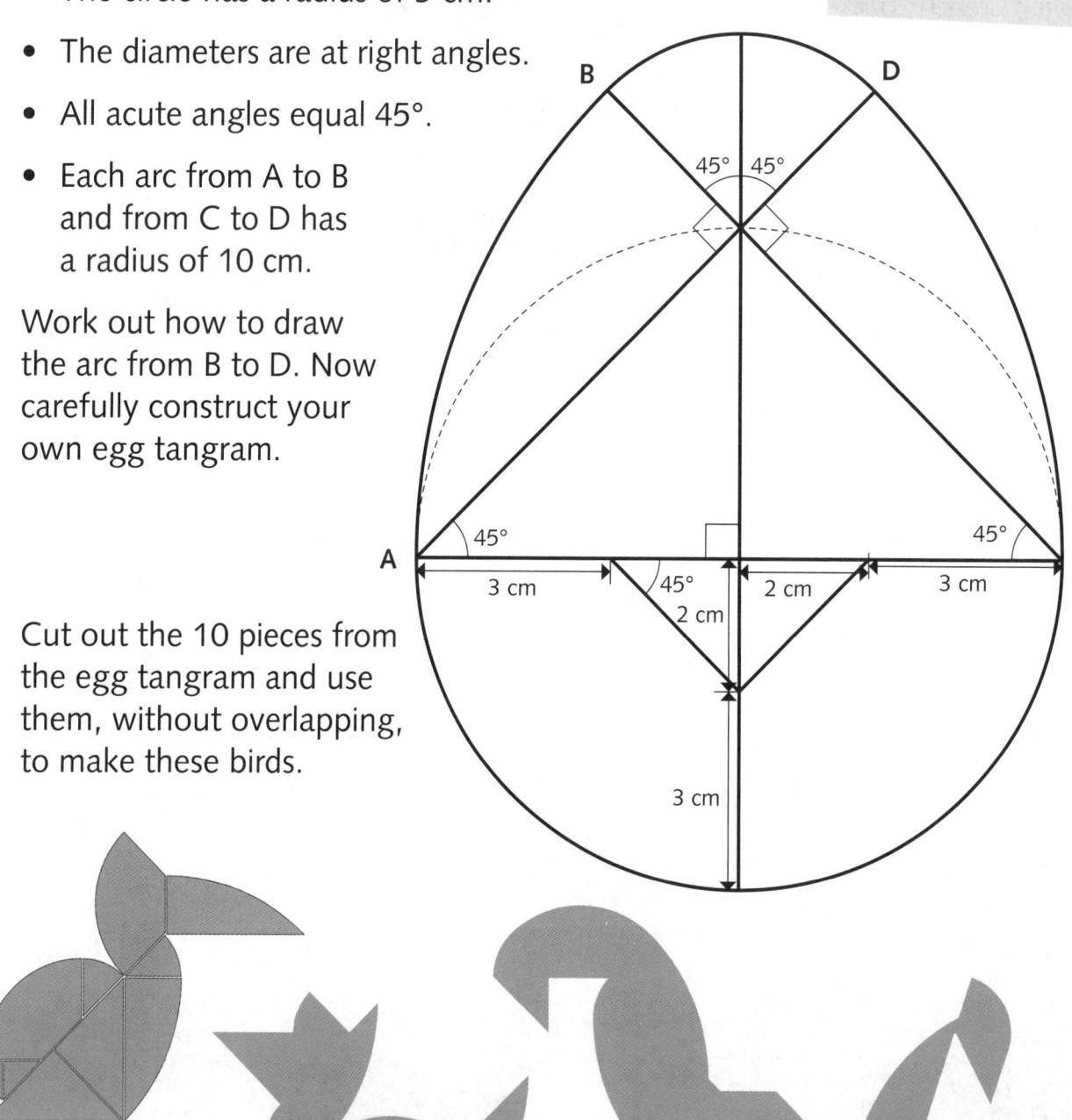

2 Cut out the 10 pieces from the egg tangram and use them, without overlapping, to make these birds.

Hint
Some pieces need to be turned over to make these birds

Name: _____ Date: _____

Multiplying decimals by a 2-digit number using the grid method

- Multiply a decimal by a 2-digit number using the grid method
- Estimate and check the answer to a calculation

Work out the answer to these calculations using the grid method.
Estimate your answer first.

Example

$2.64 \times 38 \rightarrow$ 3 × 40 = 120

x	2	0·6	0·04	
30	60	18	1·2	79·20
8	16	4·8	0·32	+ 21·12
				+ 100·32

a 6·34 × 15 →

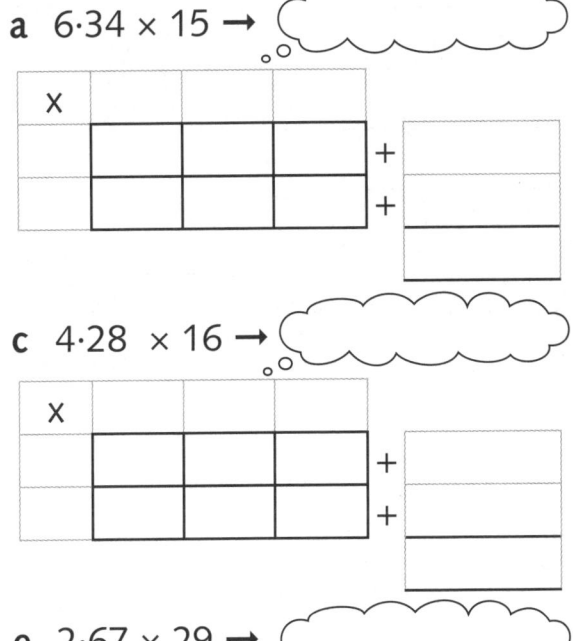

b 3·65 × 19 →

c 4·28 × 16 →

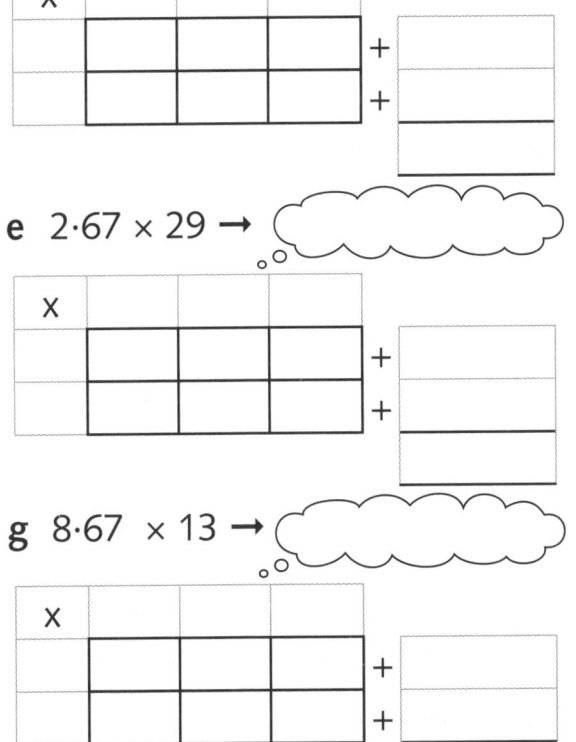

d 6·43 × 23 →

e 2·67 × 29 →

f 9·27 × 36 →

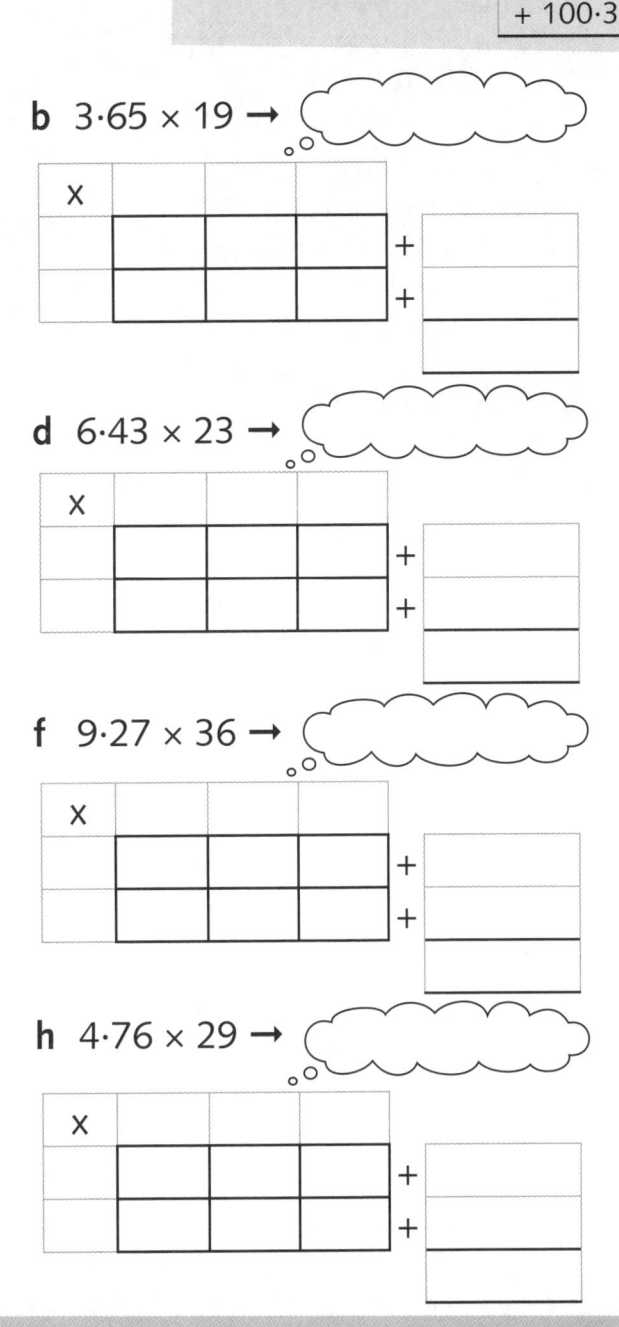

g 8·67 × 13 →

h 4·76 × 29 →

Name: _____ Date: _____

Multiplying decimals by a 2-digit number using the expanded written method

- Multiply a decimal by a 2-digit number using the expanded written method of long multiplication
- Estimate and check the answer to a calculation

Work out the answer to these calculations using the expanded written method of long multiplication. Estimate the answer first. Convert the decimals to whole numbers, carry out the calculation, then convert the answer back to a decimal.

Example

$5.37 \times 33 \rightarrow$

$(5 \times 30 = 150)$

			5	3	7	
x				3	3	
		1	6¹	1²	1	(537 × 3)
	1	6¹	1²	1	0	(537 × 30)
	1	7	7	2	1	

5.37×33 is equivalent to $537 \times 33 \div 100$.
This equals $17\ 721 \div 100$, which is 177.21.
$5.37 \times 33 = 177.21$

a $3.37 \times 15 \rightarrow$
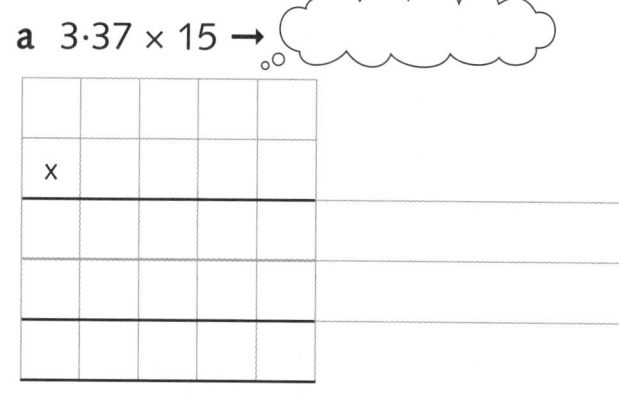

b $5.75 \times 23 \rightarrow$
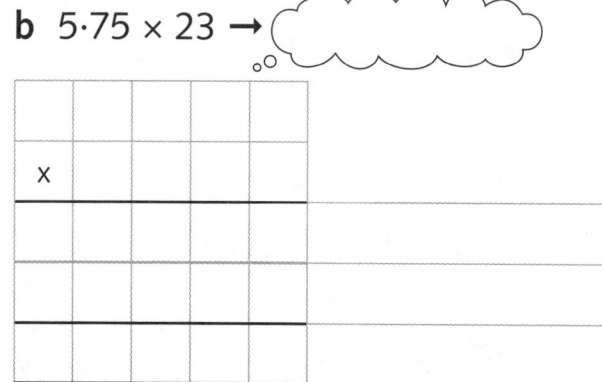

c $4.59 \times 25 \rightarrow$
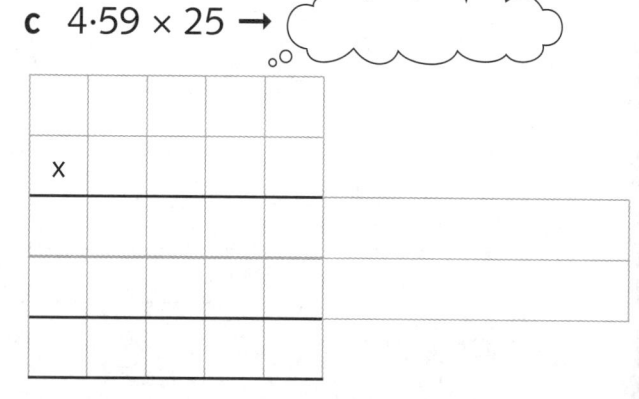

d $6.48 \times 18 \rightarrow$
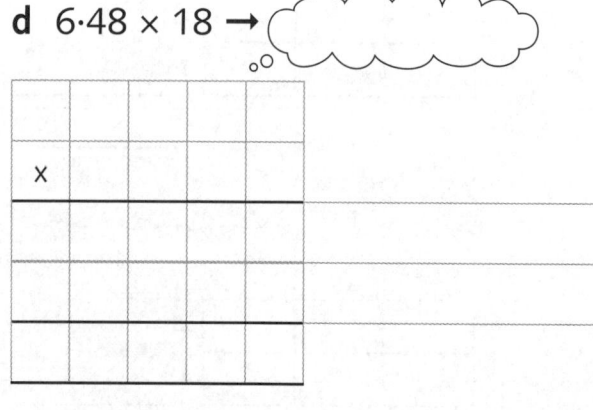

e $9.27 \times 29 \rightarrow$
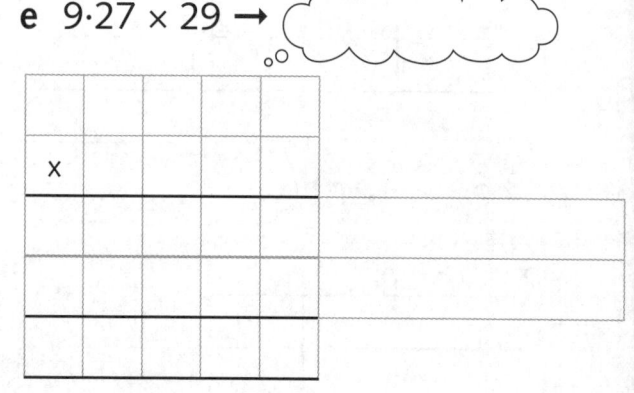

Name: _____ Date: _____

Multiplying decimals by a 2-digit number using the expanded written method

Multiply a decimal by a 2-digit number using the expanded written method of long multiplication

You will need:
- 12 counters
- 2 x 0–9 dice
- pencil and paper
- calculator

Play this game with a partner.
- Cover the price of each item on the board with a counter.
- Take turns to:
  - remove a counter from the board
  - roll the two dice and create a 2-digit number
  - multiply the cost of the item by your 2-digit number using the expanded written method
  - say the answer to the calculation. Your partner should check the answer using a calculator.
- If you are correct, keep the counter. If you are incorrect, put the counter back on the board.
- Continue until all the counters have been removed.

The player with the most counters at the end is the winner.

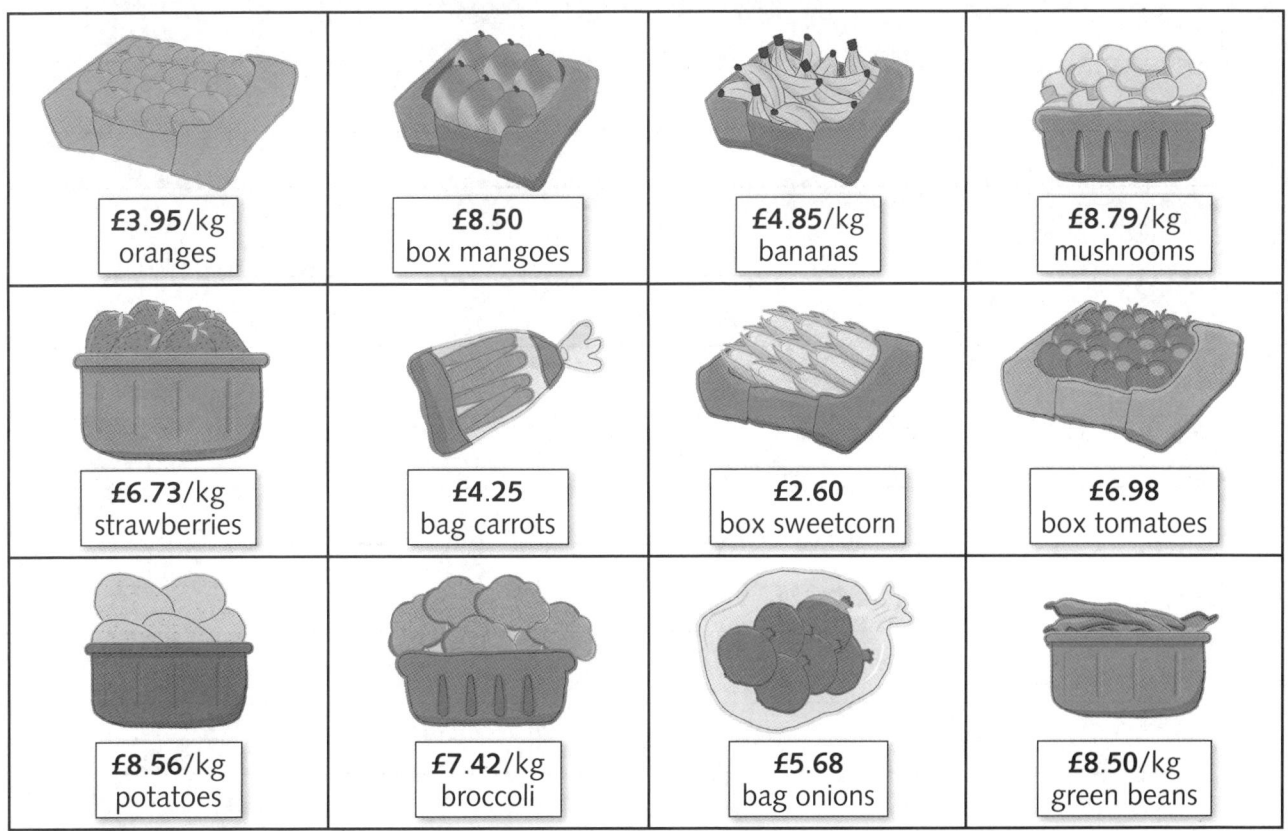

£3.95/kg oranges	£8.50 box mangoes	£4.85/kg bananas	£8.79/kg mushrooms
£6.73/kg strawberries	£4.25 bag carrots	£2.60 box sweetcorn	£6.98 box tomatoes
£8.56/kg potatoes	£7.42/kg broccoli	£5.68 bag onions	£8.50/kg green beans

Name: _____ Date: _____

Solving word problems

Solve problems involving addition, subtraction, multiplication and division

1 Use the picture to help you
write your own word problems.
Include calculations that involve
addition, subtraction,
multiplication, division or
even percentages.

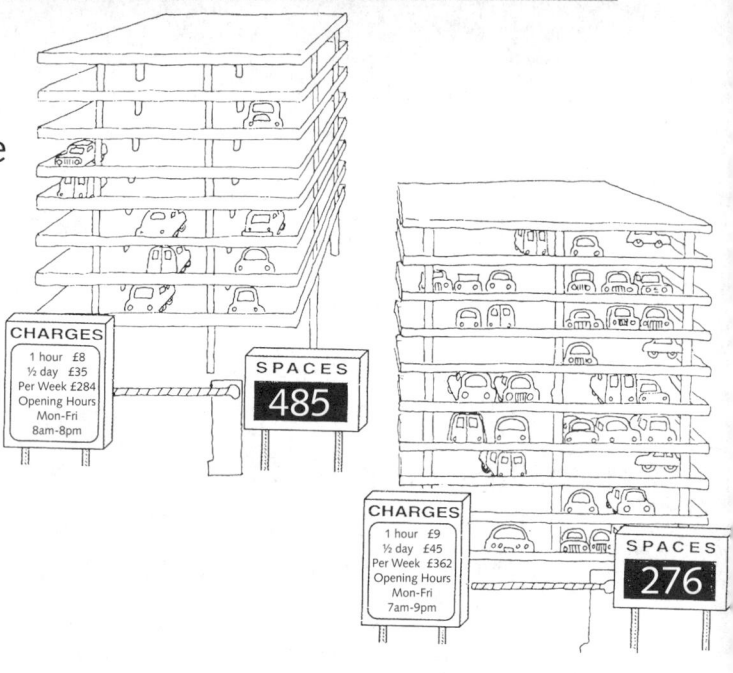

CHARGES
1 hour £8
½ day   £35
Per Week £284
Opening Hours
Mon-Fri
8am-8pm

SPACES
485

2 Calculate the answers to your
problems on the back of
this sheet.

CHARGES
1 hour £9
½ day   £45
Per Week £362
Opening Hours
Mon-Fri
7am-9pm

SPACES
276

3 Give your word problems to
a partner to solve, then check
their answers.

Name: _____ Date: _____

qual fractions

Use common multiples to express fractions in the same denomination

1 Change each of these fractions to four different fractions that are equivalent.

> **Hint**
> The numerator must be multiplied by the same number that you multiply the denominator by.

a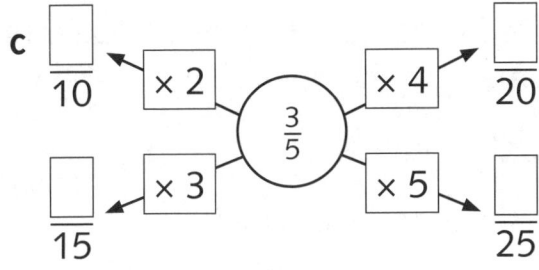

b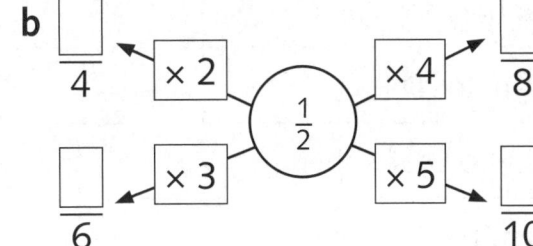

c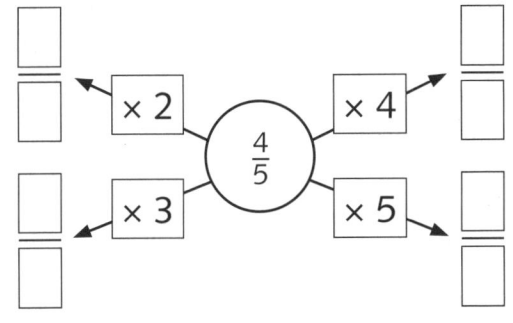

d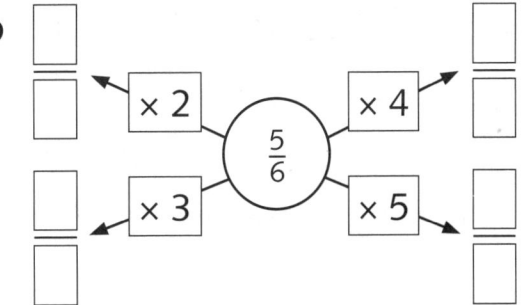

2 Change each of these fractions to four different fractions that are equivalent. This time work out the numerator and the denominator.

a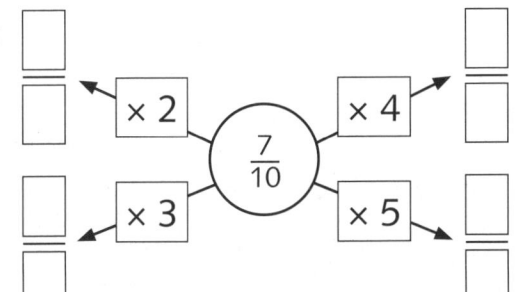

b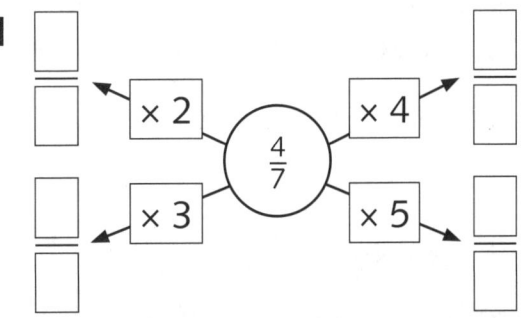

c

d

Name: _____   Date: _____

Charity spending

Solve problems involving the four operations, including calculating with fractions

You will need:
• ruler
• coloured pencils

1 One year, a charity had an annual income of £56 800.
The table below shows when in the year all of their income was spent.
Complete the table.

Months	Fraction of Total Amount	Amount Spent
January to March	$\frac{1}{5}$	
April to June	$\frac{3}{16}$	
July to September	$\frac{7}{20}$	
October to December		

2 The following year the charity wanted to increase its income by one tenth. If it
spends the same fraction per quarter, what will the new amounts spent be?

January to March   £ [   ]   April to June   £ [   ]

July to September   £ [   ]   October to December   £ [   ]

3 The Charity Manager wants a pie chart
to present the spending for each quarter.
Fill in the diagram to create one for her.

Hint
You may need to do some
rounding up and down.

4 This is how the charity received its income.
How much was raised by each source?
What fraction was raised by sponsored events?

$\frac{1}{8}$ street collections   £ [   ] $\frac{2}{5}$ charity shops   £ [   ]

$\frac{5}{16}$ donations   £ [   ]

$\frac{\boxed{}}{\boxed{}}$ sponsored events   £ [   ] $\frac{3}{20}$ fun runs   £ [   ]

Name: _____ Date: _____

raction and decimal multiplication grid

Multiply simple pairs of proper fractions, writing the answer in its simplest form

The fractions and decimals in the boxes along the top and down the left-hand side are multiplied together to make the answers in the grid.

Fill in the missing fractions.

Use the answers that have already been filled in to find the missing fractions along the top and down the left-hand side. Then work out the remaining answers.

X	0.6		$\frac{4}{7}$	0.5	
$\frac{3}{5}$		$\frac{1}{5}$			
			$\frac{8}{21}$	$\frac{1}{3}$	$\frac{5}{12}$
	$\frac{3}{25}$				
0.75		$\frac{1}{4}$			$\frac{15}{32}$

Name: _____ Date: _____

Share it out

Divide proper fractions by whole numbers

Solve these problems by dividing the fractions. Use the diagrams to help you.
Show any working out on the back of this sheet.

a Gemma has a piece of string. She cuts it so that she has $\frac{1}{2}$ of it and gives the rest to her brother. She uses her part to tie up four plants in her garden. What fraction of the original length of string does she use on each plant?

Hint
Think what fraction of the *whole* is each part.

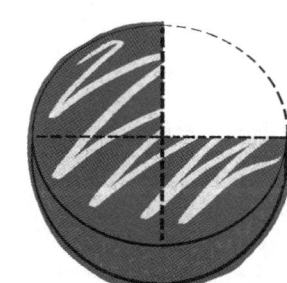

b The Cooper family have $\frac{3}{4}$ of a cake left. They want to share it out equally between four of them. What fraction of the whole cake will each of them get?

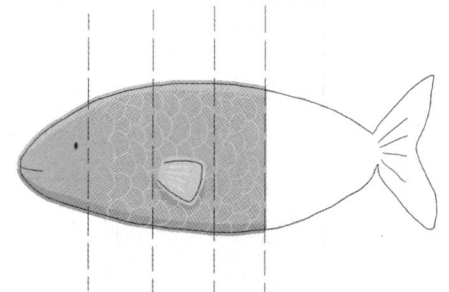

c Two cats have found $\frac{2}{3}$ of a fish to share. How much of a whole fish will each of them get?

d Mrs Billam has asked three children to stay in at lunch time to discuss their maths. She has half an hour with them. What fraction of an hour will each child have if she sees them individually?

e Colin the cook has $\frac{3}{5}$ of a bag of flour. He uses it to make two pancakes. What fraction of the a whole bag of flour is in each pancake?

Name: _____ Date: _____

ecision tree litres

Convert between millilitres and litres using decimals up to 3 places

A 0·175 *l*   **C** 0·285 *l*   **E** 0·7 *l*   **G** 0·33 *l*

    B 0·38 *l*   **D** 0·085 *l*   **F** 0·57 *l*   **H** 0·03 *l*

Use the decision tree to find which box matches the capacity of each container A to H. Then write the letter of the container in the box.

Capacity greater than 300 ml

Yes →   No →

Capacity greater than 500 ml	Capacity greater than 100 ml

Yes   No   Yes   No

Capacity greater than 500 ml	Capacity greater than 350 ml	Capacity greater than 200 ml	Capacity greater than 50 ml

Yes   No   Yes   No   Yes   No   Yes   No

Box 1	Box 2	Box 3	Box 4	Box 5	Box 6	Box 7	Box 8

Name: _____ Date: _____

Water-flow rates

Convert between units of capacity to solve problems using decimal notation

You will need:
• wide-necked jar
• measuring cylinder with 10 ml divisions
• funnel
• stopwatch
• access to water tap

An activity for two people

1 Set the water to run from the tap at a rate you would use to fill a glass of water. Set the timer. Use the wide-necked jar to collect the water for 5 seconds. Pour the water through the funnel into the measuring cylinder. Record the capacity to the nearest 10 ml in column 3 of the table.

2 Using different flow-rates, repeat the collection of water two more times. Record your results in the table.

3 For rows 1 to 3 in the table, work out how much water you would collect in 1 minute. Record your answers in column 5 of the table.

	Time (s)	Water collected (ml)	Time (min)	Water collected (ml)	
	5	80	1	960 ml	← Exampl
1	5		1		
2	5		1		
3	5		1		

4 For each water-flow rate you recorded in the above table, find how long it would take to fill a 1 litre jug. Round each answer to 1 decimal place.

	Water collected in 5 seconds	Time taken to collect 1 litre	
1	ml	min	s
2	ml	min	s
3	ml	min	s

Example

80 ml in 5 s

10 ml in $\frac{5}{8}$ s

1000 ml in $(100 \times 5) \div 8$ s

1000 ml in 62·5 s

1 l in 1 min 2·5 s

Name: _____ Date: _____

olume of cuboids

Calculate the volume of cuboids using the rule $V = lbh$

Each cuboid is made with 1 cm³ cubes.

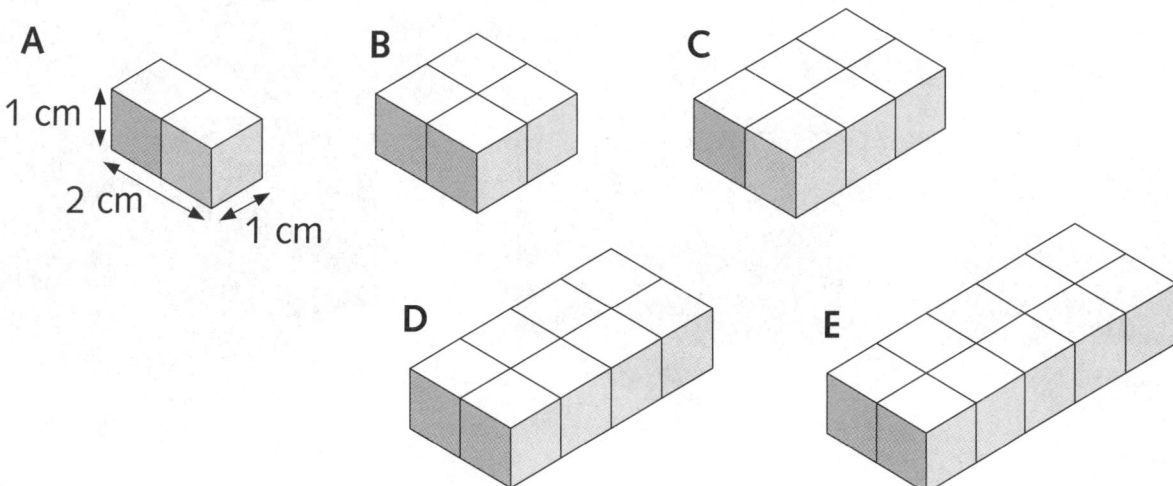

1 For each cuboid:
- write its length, breadth and height in the table
- calculate its volume in cubic centimetres (cm³).

Cuboid	Length (cm)	Breadth (cm)	Width (cm)	Volume (cm³)
A	1	2	1	2
B				
C				
D				
E				

2 Look for a pattern in the table above. Use the pattern to find the volume of the next two cuboids, F and G, in the sequence. Complete the table below.

Cuboid	Length (cm)	Breadth (cm)	Width (cm)	Volume (cm³)
F				
G				

Name: _____ Date: _____

Investigating painted cubes

Calculate and compare the volume of cubes using cubic centimetres (cm³)

Each cube is built with 1 cm³ cubes.

A   B   C

1 Calculate the volume in cubic centimetres (cm³) of cubes A, B and C. Record your answers in the table below.

2 The six faces of each cube have been painted blue. For each cube, write in the table below the number of faces of the smaller cubes that have:

- 3 faces painted blue
- 2 faces painted blue
- 1 face painted blue
- 0 faces painted blue

Cube	Volume (cm³)	Number of faces painted				Total number of cubes
		3	2	1	0	
A						
B						
C						
D						

3 Look for a pattern in each column and use it to find the answers for cube D which has dimensions of 6 cm.

Name: _____ Date: _____

ODMAS challenge

Use knowledge of the order of operations to carry out calculations involving the four operations

| 1 | 2 | 3 | 4 | 5 | 6 | 7 | 8 | 9 |

| + | − | × | ÷ | 2 |

1 Write down ten different calculations using all of the digits and operations in each one.

Hint
Don't forget to use brackets!

- What is the highest answer you can make?

- What is the lowest positive integer answer you can make?

- Can you make ten different answers?

2 Explain how you know that your highest answer is the highest possible.

_____

_____

_____

Name: _____ Date: _____

Make it to twenty

Use knowledge of the order of operations to carry out calculations involving the four operations

Can you make all the numbers from 1 to 20 using the four operations, brackets, and the number 2?

Example

$(2 \times 2 \times 2) + (2 \div 2) = 9$

Use the number 2 as many times as you need to. You can also use each of the four operations more than once and have more than one set of brackets.

You can use 22 too!

Record your calculations below, and show your working out on the back of this sheet.

1		11	
2		12	
3		13	
4		14	
5		15	
6		16	
7		17	
8		18	
9		19	
10		20	

Name: _____ Date: _____

Make the puzzle

Solve problems involving addition, subtraction, multiplication and division

Write the clues for this number puzzle. Use the top grid for your answers. When it is complete, cut along the lines and give the blank grid and the clues to a partner to work out.

Across

1	
5	
8	
9	
10	
12	
15	
18	
20	
23	
25	
26	
27	

Down

2	
3	
4	
5	
6	
7	
11	
13	
14	
16	
17	
19	
21	
22	
24	

Name: _____ Date: _____

Another curious question

Solve problems involving addition, subtraction, multiplication and division

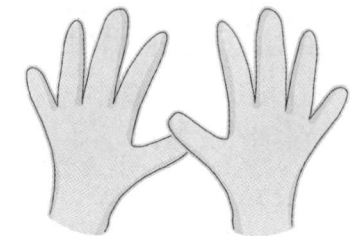

- How long is 100 000 seconds?

- How far would 100 000 hand spans stretch?

- How many cups would 100 000 counters fill?

- How long would it take you to write your name 100 000 times?

Choose one question to answer. Use this space for your working out.

Working out

Name: _____ Date: _____

atio generator

You will need:
• 1–6 dice

- Understand and use ratio to solve problems
- Solve problems involving scale factors

This is a game for two players. This grid is the ratio generator.

Second dice						
6	16	1	15	24	11	5
5	21	8	4	wild card	wild card	14
4	wild card	19	9	17	6	12
3	12	wild card	wild card	10	23	18
2	3	12	2	12	12	wild card
1	7	20	12	13	22	25
	1	2	3	4	5	6

First dice

- Each player rolls the dice twice to find coordinates of a square. This is your first number.

- If you land on a wild card, you can choose your own number.

- Each player rolls the dice two more times to find coordinates of another square. This is your second number.

- Find the ratio between your two numbers. Simplify the ratio if you can.

- Each make up and write down a ratio word problem that uses these two numbers.

- Swap papers and try and answer each other's questions.

- Play for 10 minutes.

Example

You roll a 3 and 6. This gives you coordinates (3, 6) which is 15.
Then you roll a 2 and 2. This gives you coordinate (2, 2) which is 12.
Your ratio is 15 : 12 that simplifies to become 5 : 4. Question: A market gardener plants red and yellow rose bushes in the ratio 5 : 4. If he plants 50 red bushes, how many yellow bushes does he plant?

Name: _____ Date: _____

Egg ratios and proportions

Use knowledge of fractions and multiples to solve ratio and proportion problems

A farmer keeps 150 hens for eggs. Every day he collects the eggs and sorts them into size: small (S), medium (M) and large (L). Here is his record of the eggs laid by his hens for one week.

Days of the week	Small	Medium	Large	Total
Sunday	40	60	20	
Monday	50	50	25	
Tuesday	30	50	40	
Wednesday	30	50	50	
Thursday	35	70	35	
Friday	20	50	50	
Saturday	30	60	40	

1 a Calculate the total number of eggs laid each day and write this in the table.

b On which day were the most eggs laid? _____

c On which days were the least number of eggs laid? _____

2 a Calculate the ratio of S : M : L for each day in its simplest form.

Day of the week	small: medium: large
Sunday	
Monday	
Tuesday	
Wednesday	
Thursday	
Friday	
Saturday	

b Calculate the proportion of large eggs for each day as a fraction.

Day of the week	Proportion of large eggs
Sunday	
Monday	
Tuesday	
Wednesday	
Thursday	
Friday	
Saturday	

3 On which day did the hens lay the biggest proportion of large eggs?

_____

4 On the back of this sheet, write a ratio or proportion question of your own and try it out on a friend.

Name: _____ Date: _____

aper sizes

Understand and use ratio to solve problems

Use a calculator to find the ratios of length to width (L : W) to 1 decimal place.

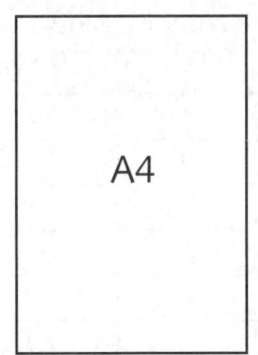

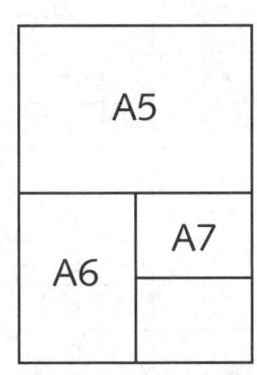

You will need:
- A4 sheet of paper
- A3 sheet of paper
- calculator
- ruler
- scissors

1 Measure an A4 sheet of paper carefully to the nearest millimetre.

Length = [   ]   Width = [   ]   L (A4) : W (A4) = [   ] : [   ]

2 Fold the A4 sheet so that it is A5 size and cut it in half along the fold. Measure the A5 sheet carefully to the nearest millimetre.

Length = [   ]   Width = [   ]   L (A5) : W(5) = [   ] : [   ]

3 Fold the A5 sheet so that is it A6 size and cut it in half along the fold. Measure the A6 sheet carefully to the nearest millimetre.

Length = [   ]   Width = [   ]   L (A6) : W(6) = [   ] : [   ]

4 a What do you notice about the length to width ratios for A4, A5 and A6?

_____

b Use this knowledge to predict the length and width of A7 paper.

L (A7) = [   ] mm   W (A7) = [   ] mm

5 Predict the ratio L (A3) : W (A3).
Now measure the length and width of the A3 sheet of paper and calculate the ratio. L (A3) : W (A3) = [   ] : [   ]

Was your prediction correct? _____

Name: _____ Date: _____

Theme park ratios

- Understand and use ratio to solve problems
- Solve problems involving scale factors

Here are some statistics for rides at a theme park.

Name of ride	Height (m)	Length (m)	Top speed (km/h)	Max angle (°)	Inversions (complete turns)	No. of carriages	Riders per carriage	Total no. of riders
Breeze (B)	20	800	75	40	2	1	24	
Downfall (D)	14	700	80	40	4	2	32	
Nihility (N)	20	400	105	90	0	3	16	
Random (R)	22	600	100	50	0	4	20	
Escape (E)	20	300	35	30	0	6	32	
Xtreme (X)	18	800	65	70	0	8	20	

Use the table to answer these ratio problems. Give each ratio in its simplest form. Use the back of this sheet for any working.

1 Find the ratios of ride heights.

B : D : N : R : E : X = ☐ : ☐ : ☐ : ☐ : ☐ : ☐

2 Find the ratio of the longest ride to the shortest ride.

longest : shortest = ☐ : ☐

3 Find the ratio of the fastest ride to the slowest ride.

fastest : slowest = ☐ : ☐

4 Find the ratio of inversions for Breeze to Downfall.

B : D = ☐ : ☐

5 Find the ratio of riders per carriage

B : D : N : R : E : X = ☐ : ☐ : ☐ : ☐ : ☐ : ☐

6 Fill in the total number of riders in the final column of the table and calculate the ratio of total riders per ride.

B : D : N : R : E : X = ☐ : ☐ : ☐ : ☐ : ☐ : ☐

7 Which ride do you think makes the biggest profit for the Theme Park?

Explain your choice._____

_____

8 Which ride would you like best? Explain your choice on the back of this sheet.

Name: _____ Date: _____

ocate the shapes

Use coordinates to describe the position of shapes in all four quadrants

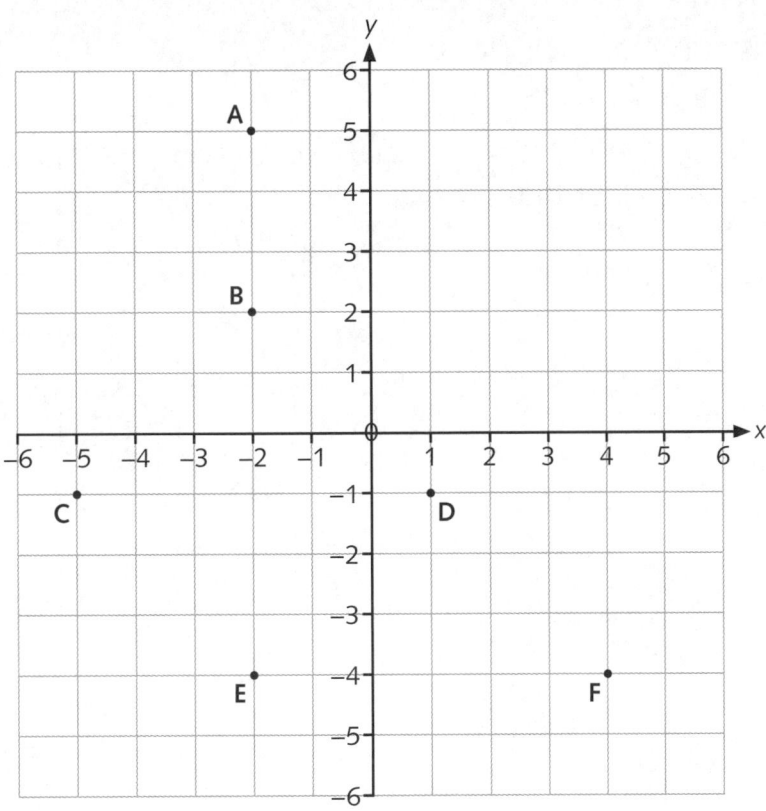

1 List the coordinates of the vertices that form:

   a a square   (____ , ____) (____ , ____) (____ , ____) (____ , ____)

   b a parallelogram (____ , ____) (____ , ____) (____ , ____) (____ , ____)

   c a kite   (____ , ____) (____ , ____) (____ , ____) (____ , ____)

   d a trapezium   (____ , ____) (____ , ____) (____ , ____) (____ , ____)

2 List the coordinates of a non-right-angled isosceles triangle.
   (____ , ____) (____ , ____) (____ , ____)

3 The points D (1, −1) and E (−2, −4) are two vertices of a right-angled isosceles triangle. Find two different coordinates for the third vertex.
   (_____ , _____) (_____ , _____)

4 AE and EF are two sides of a rectangle. Write the coordinates of the vertex
   G. (_____ , _____)

Name: _____ Date: _____

Points on the run

Use coordinates to describe the position of shapes in all four quadrants

You are competing in a cross country race. At each checkpoint on the course you collect a letter of the alphabet.

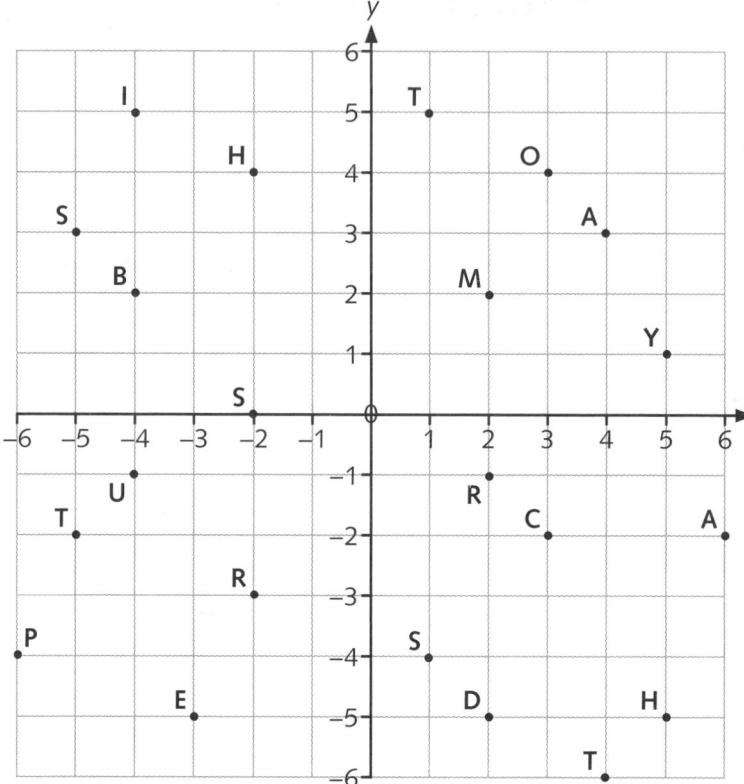

1 Find the code letter for each of your checkpoints in the Code Grid.

Checkpoint	(2, 2)	(4, 3)	(1, 5)	(−2, 4)	(−5, 3)
Code letter					

Checkpoint	(−2, 0)	(−4, −1)	(−6, −4)	(−3, −5)	(−2, −3)
Code letter					

Checkpoint	(1, −4)	(4, −6)	(6, −2)	(2, −1)
Code letter				

2 The course starts and finishes at (0, 0). Join your checkpoints in order, starting and finishing at (0, 0).

3 On the back of this sheet, use the Code Grid to write a secret message for a partner to crack.

Name: _____ Date: _____

On reflection

Use coordinates to reflect shapes into all four quadrants

1 Reflect the shape in the *y*-axis, then reflect the shape and its image in the *x*-axis.

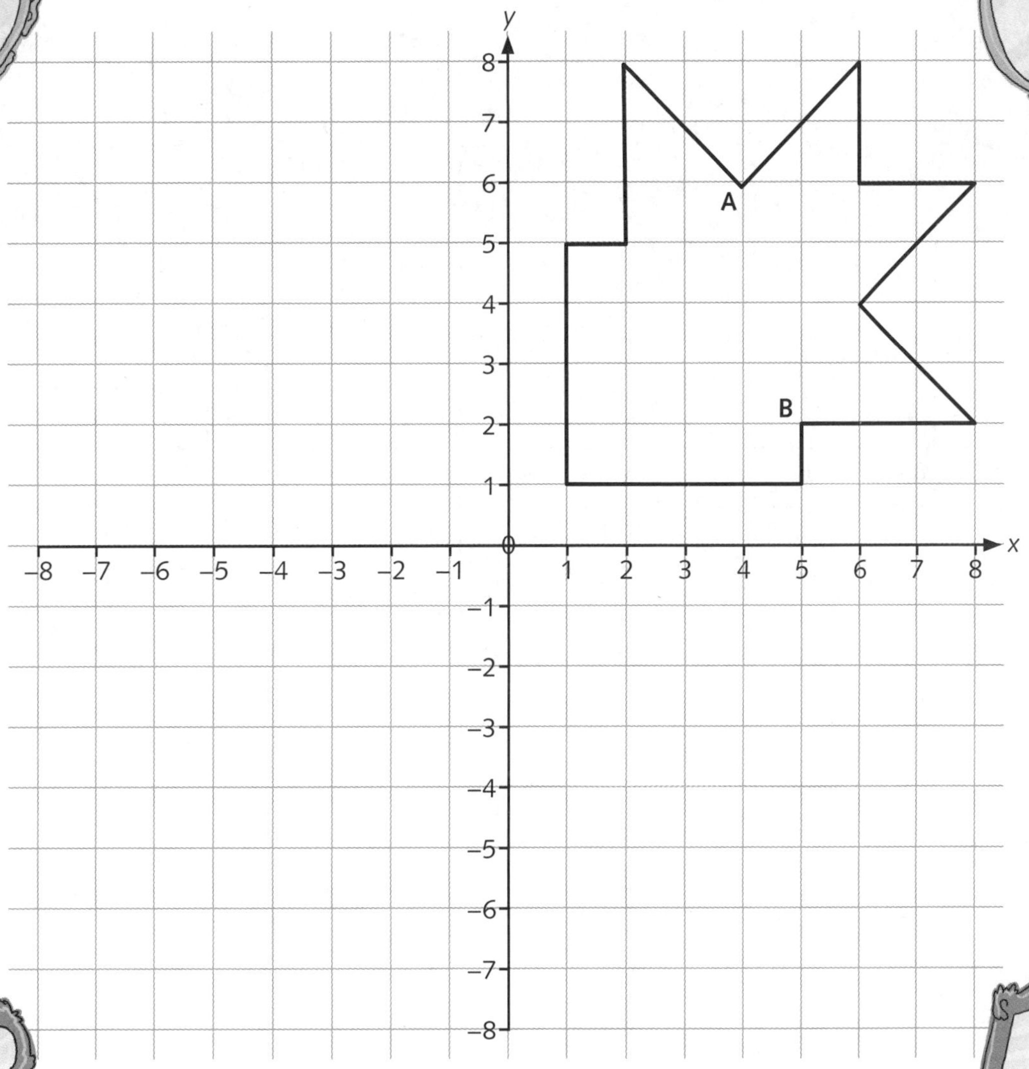

2 Write the coordinates of the images of points A and B in the table.

First quadrant	Second quadrant	Third quadrant	Fourth quadrant
A (4, 6)	A' (,)	A'' (,)	A''' (,)
B (5, 2)	B' (,)	B'' (,)	B''' (,)

Name: _____ Date: _____

4-quadrant pattern

Use coordinates to reflect shapes into all four quadrants

1 Reflect the shape in the *y*-axis, then reflect the shape and its image in the *x*-axis

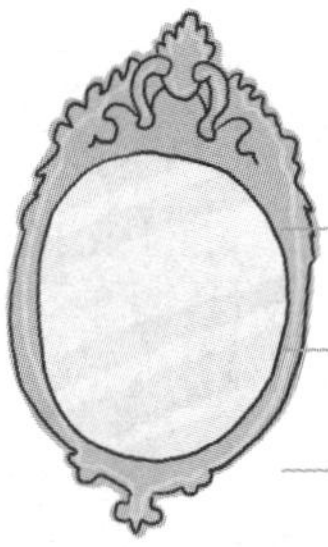

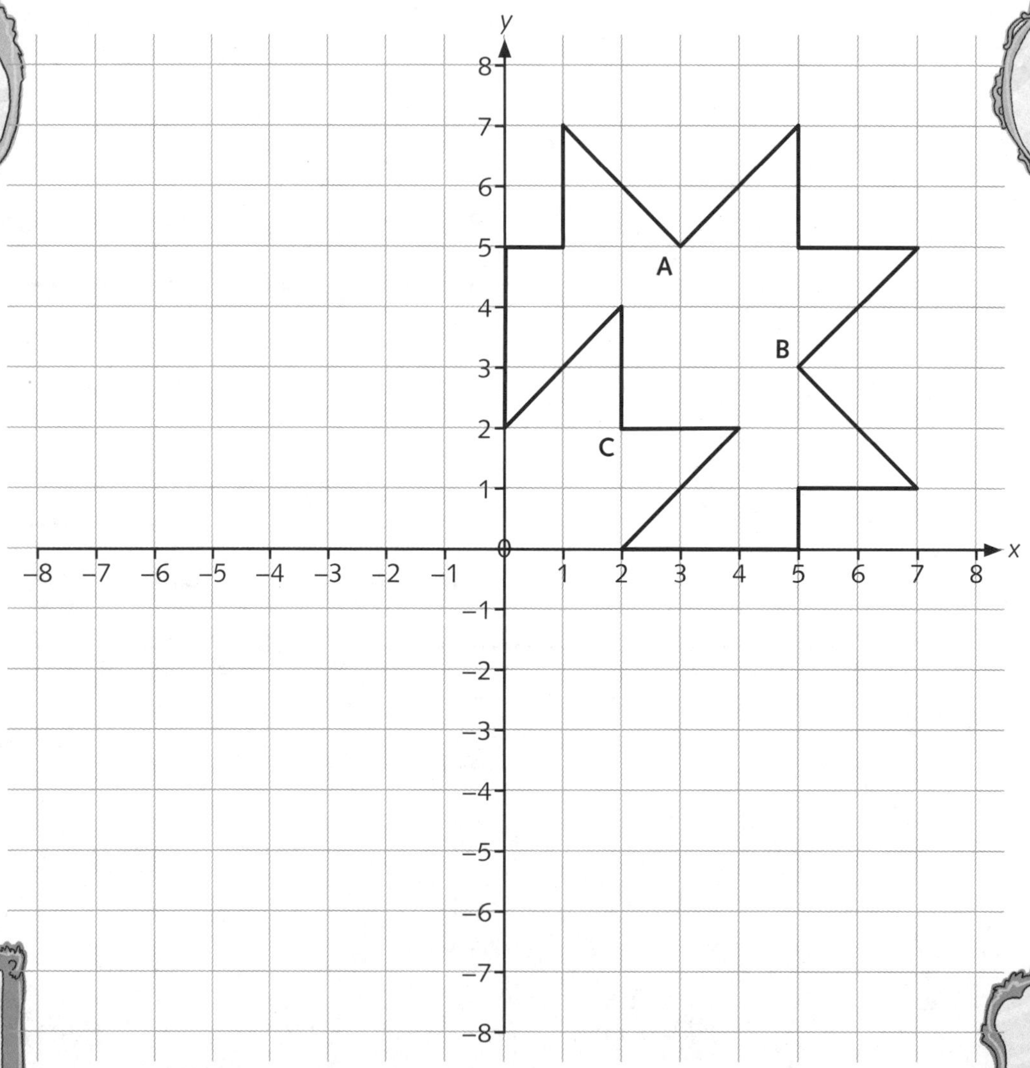

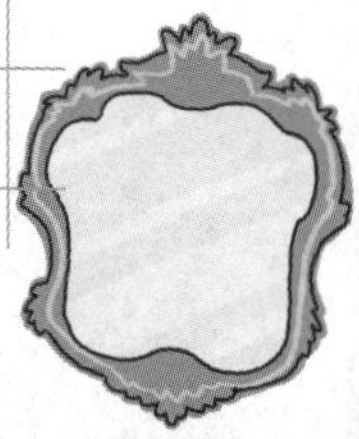

2 a Write the coordinates of the points A, B and C in the table.
b Write the coordinates of the images of points A, B and C in the table.

First quadrant	Second quadrant	Third quadrant	Fourth quadrant
A (,)	A' (,)	A'' (,)	A''' (,)
B (,)	B' (,)	B'' (,)	B''' (,)
C (,)	C' (,)	C'' (,)	C''' (,)

Name: _____ Date: _____

Using divisibility tests

Use knowledge of multiples and factors to conduct tests of divisibility

You will need:
• coloured pencils

| 2 | 3 | 4 | 5 | 6 | 8 | 9 | 10 | 25 |

1 Use the numbers on the cards above to complete these rules.

A number is divisible by ☐ if the sum of its digits is divisible by 3.

A number is divisible by ☐ if the sum of its digits are divisible by 9.

A number is divisible by ☐ if the last two digits end in 25, 50, 75 or 00.

A number is divisible by ☐ if the tens and ones divide exactly by 4.

A number is divisible by ☐ if it is an even number and the last digit is 0, 2, 4, 6, or 8.

A number is divisible by ☐ if the last digit is 0 or 5.

A number is divisible by ☐ if half of it is divisible by 4 or if its last three digits are divisible by 8.

A number is divisible by ☐ if it is even and is also divisible by 3.

A number is divisible by ☐ if the last digit is 0 or 5.

2 In each box use the divisibility rules to find and colour in the multiples of the number shown.

Multiples of 5
327 521 680 400
625 370 745 1200

Multiples of 9
275 636 585 321
463 774 981 479

Multiples of 3
141 675 789 553
278 365 492 486

Multiples of 25
750 225 2475 1320
2050 135 6700 550

Name: _____ Date: _____

Review multiplication and division of whole numbers

- Use appropriate methods to multiply and divide whole numbers
- Estimate and check the answer to a calculation

1 Sort these calculations into two groups: those that you can calculate using mental methods and those where you need to use a written method Find the answer to each calculation using the most appropriate method..

| 5427 ÷ 9 | 48 × 56 | 3569 ÷ 6 | 5333 × 3 | 232 × 3 | 74 × 25 |

| 67 × 5 | 4998 × 8 | 3569 ÷ 6 | 768 × 7 | 9366 ÷ 3 | 4741 ÷ 11 |

Mental method	Written method

2 Write the answers to the calculations you can work out using a mental method. For the calculations that need a written method, choose one multiplication and one division calculation, and work out the answers on the back of this sheet. Remember to estimate the answer first and then use your estimate to check your answer.

Name: _____ Date: _____

Review multiplication and division of whole numbers

You will need:
• scissors
• pencil and paper (per player)

• Use appropriate methods to multiply and divide whole numbers
• Estimate and check the answer to a calculation

Work with a partner
• Cut out both sets of number cards below, keeping the sets separate.
• Shuffle each set of cards and place them face down in two piles.
• Take turns to choose a number card from each pile.
• Calculate the answer by either multiplying or dividing the numbers, using the most appropriate and most efficient method.
• Write down the calculation, any working and your answer.
• Check each other's working and answer.

Set A		Set B	
34	3467	8	16
273	159	38	9
398	58	29	84
4528	816	4	47
66	854	50	6
2760	387	3	36
47	85	99	12
639	768	11	18
409	486	68	25

Name: _____ Date: _____

Review multiplication and division involving decimal numbers

- Use appropriate methods to multiply or divide decimals
- Estimate and check the answer to a calculation

You will need:
- a catalogue of school items
- scissors
- glue
- paper clip and pencil – for spinner

- Choose 6 items from the catalogue. Copy or cut out and glue a picture of each item in the boxes below.
- Write the price of the item in the price tag.
- Spin the spinner to determine how many of each item you will buy.
- Write the calculation you will use, then estimate your answer.
- Work out the answer to the calculation using the most appropriate and efficient method.

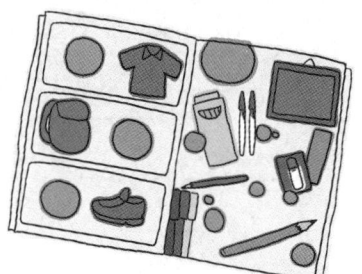

Item	Calculation , estimation and working
	Estimate:
	Estimate:
	Estimate:
	Estimate:
	Estimate:

Name: _____ Date: _____

ale prices

Solve problems involving percentages

The stationery shop is having a sale.
Some prices are reduced by 10%, some by 20% and some by 25%.
Work out the sale prices.

Reduced by 10%

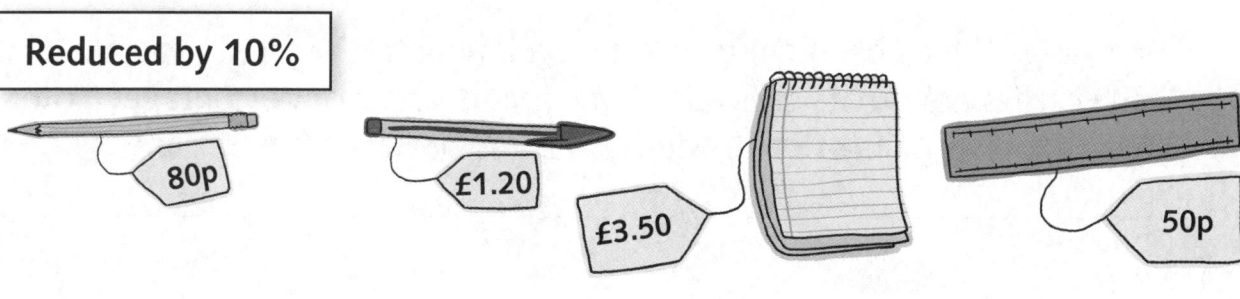

80p   £1.20   £3.50   50p

Sale price: [ ]   Sale price: [ ]   Sale price: [ ]   Sale price: [ ]

Reduced by 20%

 £4.20    £5.10    £3.70    £2.30

Sale price: [ ]   Sale price: [ ]   Sale price: [ ]   Sale price: [ ]

Reduced by 25%

 £6.80    £13   £7.40    £10.20

Sale price: [ ]   Sale price: [ ]   Sale price: [ ]   Sale price: [ ]

Name: ______________________ Date: ______________

Slide into place

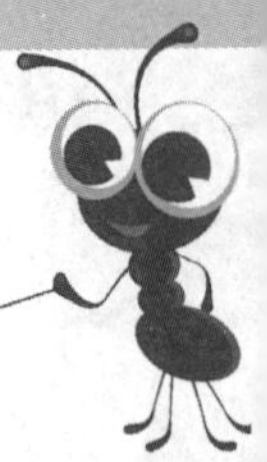

Recognise equivalences between fractions, decimals and percentages

You will need:
- scissors

- Cut out the cards below.
- Shuffle the cards and lay them face up in a 5 x 3 grid formation. One space will be empty.
- Rearrange the cards, moving one card a time into the empty space, so each card is next to its equivalent fraction, decimal or percentage. Note that as well as pairs of cards there are some groups of three cards.

$\frac{3}{8}$	0·375	75%	0·4	4%
0·125	0·81	81%	60%	25%
0·25	$\frac{3}{4}$	$\frac{1}{8}$	$\frac{3}{5}$	$\frac{1}{4}$

Name: _____ Date: _____

oint to it

Use division to convert fractions to decimals

A game for three players.

- One player is the caller.
- The other two players put their index fingers on the squares at the bottom of the sheet.
- The caller calls out one of the fractions from the box.
- The other players have to put their finger on the equivalent decimal as quickly as they can.
- The first person to point to the correct decimal scores a point.
- Keep playing until one player has scored five points.
- Then swap roles.

Do you get quicker the more you play?

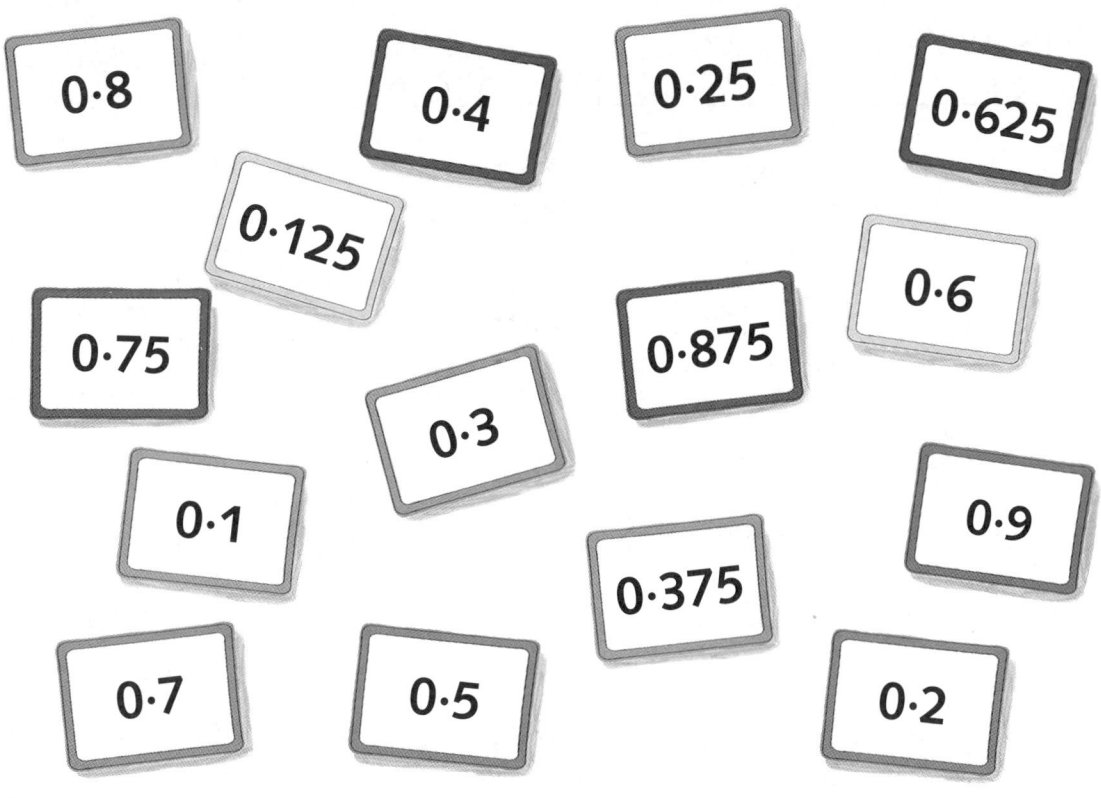

| INDEX FINGER |

| INDEX FINGER |

Column on right (top to bottom): $\frac{9}{10}$, $\frac{8}{10}$, $\frac{7}{10}$, $\frac{6}{10}$, $\frac{5}{10}$, $\frac{4}{10}$, $\frac{3}{10}$, $\frac{2}{10}$, $\frac{1}{10}$, $\frac{7}{8}$, $\frac{6}{8}$, $\frac{5}{8}$, $\frac{4}{8}$, $\frac{3}{8}$, $\frac{2}{8}$, $\frac{1}{8}$, $\frac{4}{5}$, $\frac{3}{5}$, $\frac{2}{5}$, $\frac{1}{5}$, $\frac{3}{4}$, $\frac{1}{4}$, $\frac{1}{2}$

Decimal cards: 0·8, 0·4, 0·25, 0·625, 0·125, 0·6, 0·75, 0·875, 0·3, 0·1, 0·375, 0·9, 0·7, 0·5, 0·2

Name: _____ Date: _____

Cover them up

Use division to convert fractions to decimals

You will need:
• 3 x 0-9 dice
• counters in two colours
• calculator

A game for two players.

Take turns to:
• roll the 3 dice
• use the digits to make a proper fraction. The numerator will be a 1-digit number and the denominator a 2-digit number, e.g. 9/35

• estimate the decimal equivalent of your fraction to 1 decimal place.

The other player uses the calculator to convert your fraction to a decimal and then rounds it to 1 decimal place.

If your estimate is correct, you cover the decimal on the grid with your colour counter.

The winner is the first person to get three counters in a row: vertical, horizontal or diagonal.

0	0·3	0·6	0·3	0·8	0·2
0.6	0·1	0·7	0·5	0·1	0·5
0·3	0·9	0·4	0·7	0·4	0·6
0·5	0·4	0·2	0	0·9	0·1
0·1	0·8	0·5	0·2	0·6	0
0·5	0·2	0·3	0·4	0·4	0·3

Name: _____ Date: _____

remier pie charts

Use pie charts to solve problems

The Premier Pie Company surveyed 100 customers at its shop. They asked:

> Which of our pie fillings do you like best?

They recorded the results in a percentage pie chart.

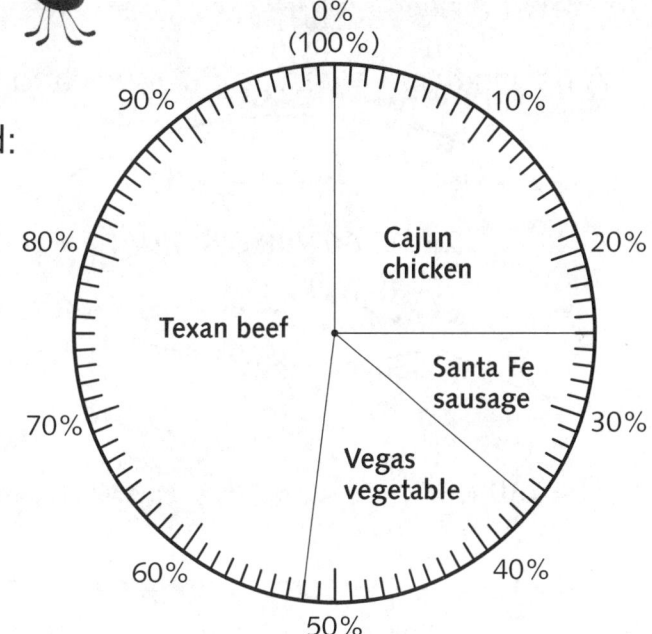

Preferred pie fillings

1 Use the information above and in the pie chart to complete the table.

Preferred pie filling	Percentage of customers	Number of customers
Cajun chicken		
Santa Fe sausage		
Vegas vegetable		
Texan beef		

2 Test each statement in turn and write whether it is true or false.

a More people prefer Cajun chicken than
Santa Fe sausage and Vegas vegetable combined.   _____

b One person in every four likes Cajun chicken best.   _____

c Beef and sausage pies are the favourite of
more than 60% of the customers.   _____

d Three times as many customers prefer Texan beef pies
as those who prefer Vegas vegetable pies.   _____

Name: _____ Date: _____

Pie chart survey

Use pie charts to solve problems

A national survey asked 500 girls and 500 boys, aged 11 to 12:

When choosing what to eat, do you consider your health?

Response	Girls (%)	Boys (%)
Always	5	5
Very often	12	9
Quite often	26	22
Sometimes	47	45
Never	10	19

The table shows how they replied.

1 Complete the percentage pie charts to show the information from the survey.

Survey of 500 girls

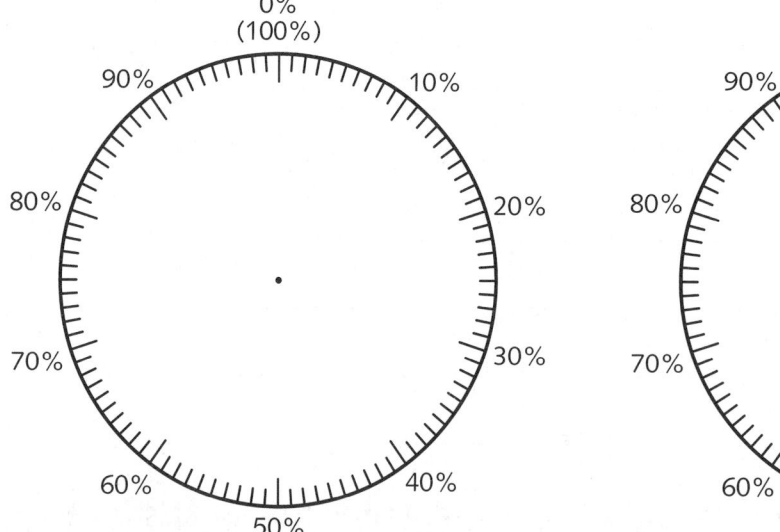

Survey of 500 boys

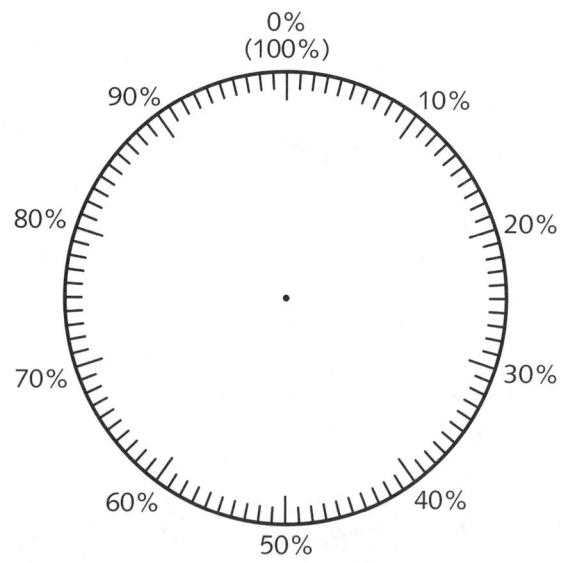

2 Test each statement in turn and write whether it is true or false.

  a Overall more girls than boys made healthy choices. _____

  b 25 out of 500 boys answered 'Always'. _____

  c Almost twice as many boys as girls answered 'Never'. _____

  d Fewer than 120 girls answered 'Quite often'. _____

3 Write one more fact that you can interpret from the pie charts.

_____

_____

Name: _____ Date: _____

bout means

Calculate and interpret the mean as an average

1 Find the mean number of eggs laid by three hens.

$(1 + 2 + 3) \div 3 =$ ⬚

2 Find the mean mass of the four parcels.

(⬚ + ⬚ + ⬚ + ⬚) kg = ⬚ kg

⬚ kg ÷ 4 = ⬚ kg

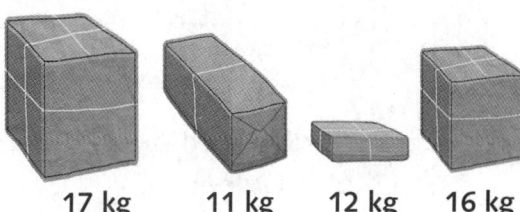

17 kg   11 kg   12 kg   16 kg

3 Find the mean height of the six trees.

(⬚ + ⬚ + ⬚ + ⬚ + ⬚ + ⬚) m = ⬚ m

⬚ m ÷ 6 = ⬚ m

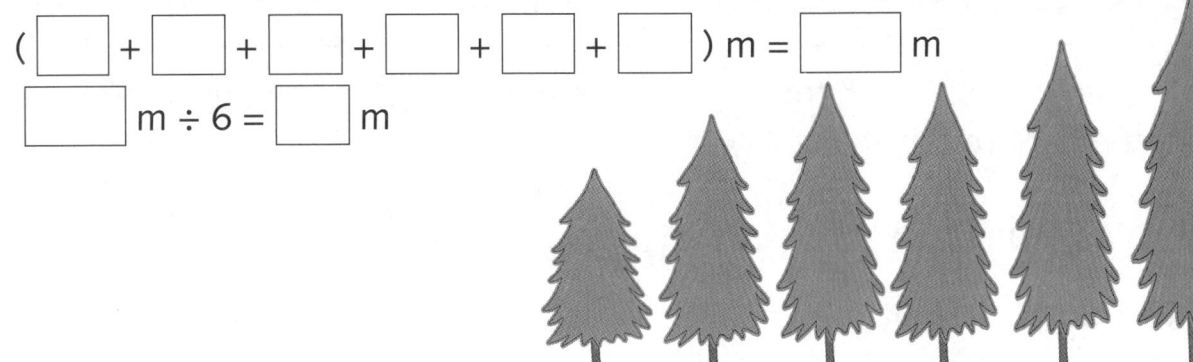

26 m   34 m   35 m   35 m   30 m   38 m

4 Find the mean amount of money in the cash boxes.

£(⬚ + ⬚ + ⬚ + ⬚) = £ ⬚

£ ⬚ ÷ 4 = £ ⬚

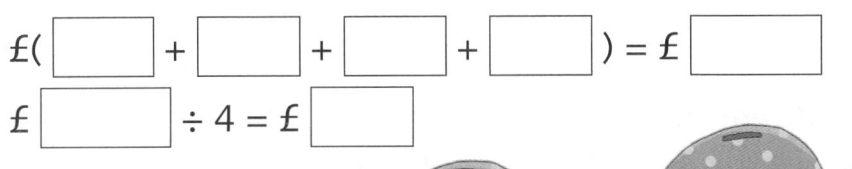

5 Find the mean of the dice throws.

Total dice throws ⬚ ÷ ⬚ = ⬚

The mean dice score is ⬚ .

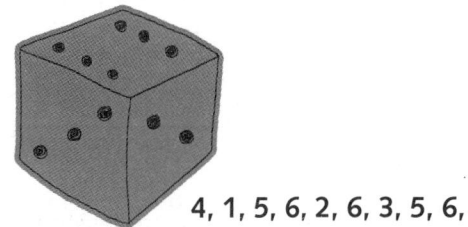

4, 1, 5, 6, 2, 6, 3, 5, 6, 2

Name: _____ Date: _____

Investigating means

Calculate and interpret the mean as an average

Step 1 Choose three different one-digit numbers. 2 3 6	Step 2 List the six three-digit numbers you can make, then add them up.	$\begin{array}{r} 236 \\ 263 \\ 326 \\ 362 \\ 623 \\ + 632 \\ \hline 2442 \end{array}$	Step 3 Find the mean of the six numbers. $2442 \div 6 = 407$
Step 4 Find the digit sum of the three numbers. $2 + 3 + 6 = 11$	Step 5 Divide the mean by the sum of the digits. $407 \div 11 = 37$		Is the answer always 37 for any set of three different 1 digit numbers? Investigate.

1 Follow Steps 2 to 5 for these sets of numbers. Record your working in full on the back of this sheet.

   a 1, 4 and 5 [   ]

   b 3, 5 and 7 [   ]

   c 3, 5 and 7 [   ]

2 Choose three more sets of three different 1-digit numbers and investigate as above. Use the back of this sheet for your calculations.

3 Write what you notice.

   _____

   _____

   _____